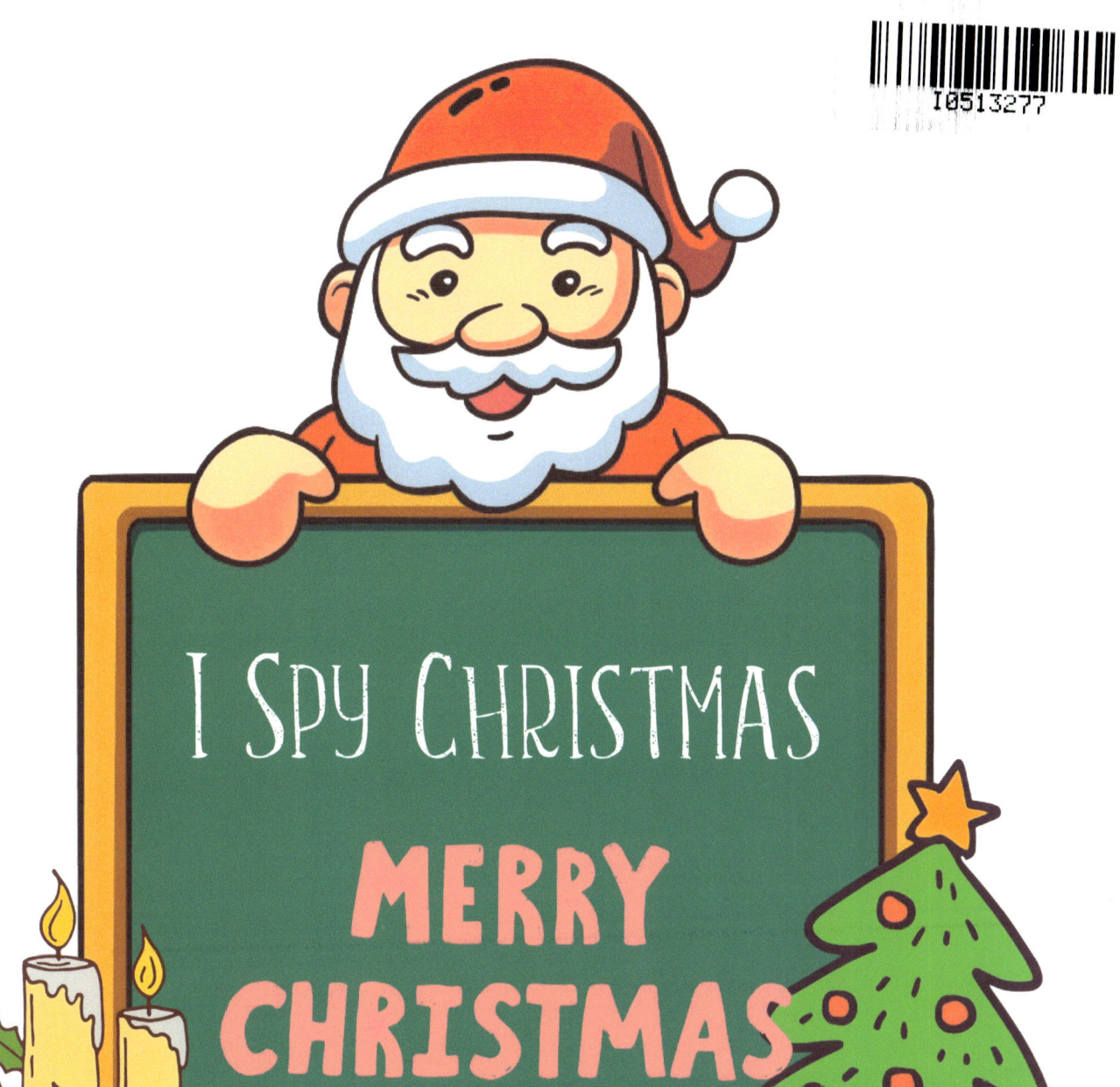

Enjoy this Notebook?

Please leave us a review as we would love to hear your reviews, thoughts, and advice in order to create better products and services for you.

Thank you for your support.

Copyright © 2019 by Little Kids Creative Press
All rights reserved. No part of this publication may be reproduced, distributed, or transmitted in any form or by any means, including photocopying, recording, or other electronic or mechanical methods, without the prior written permission of the publisher, except in the case of brief quotations embodied in critical reviews and certain other noncommercial uses permitted by copyright law.

I SPY WITH MY LITTLE EYE ...
something beginning with ...

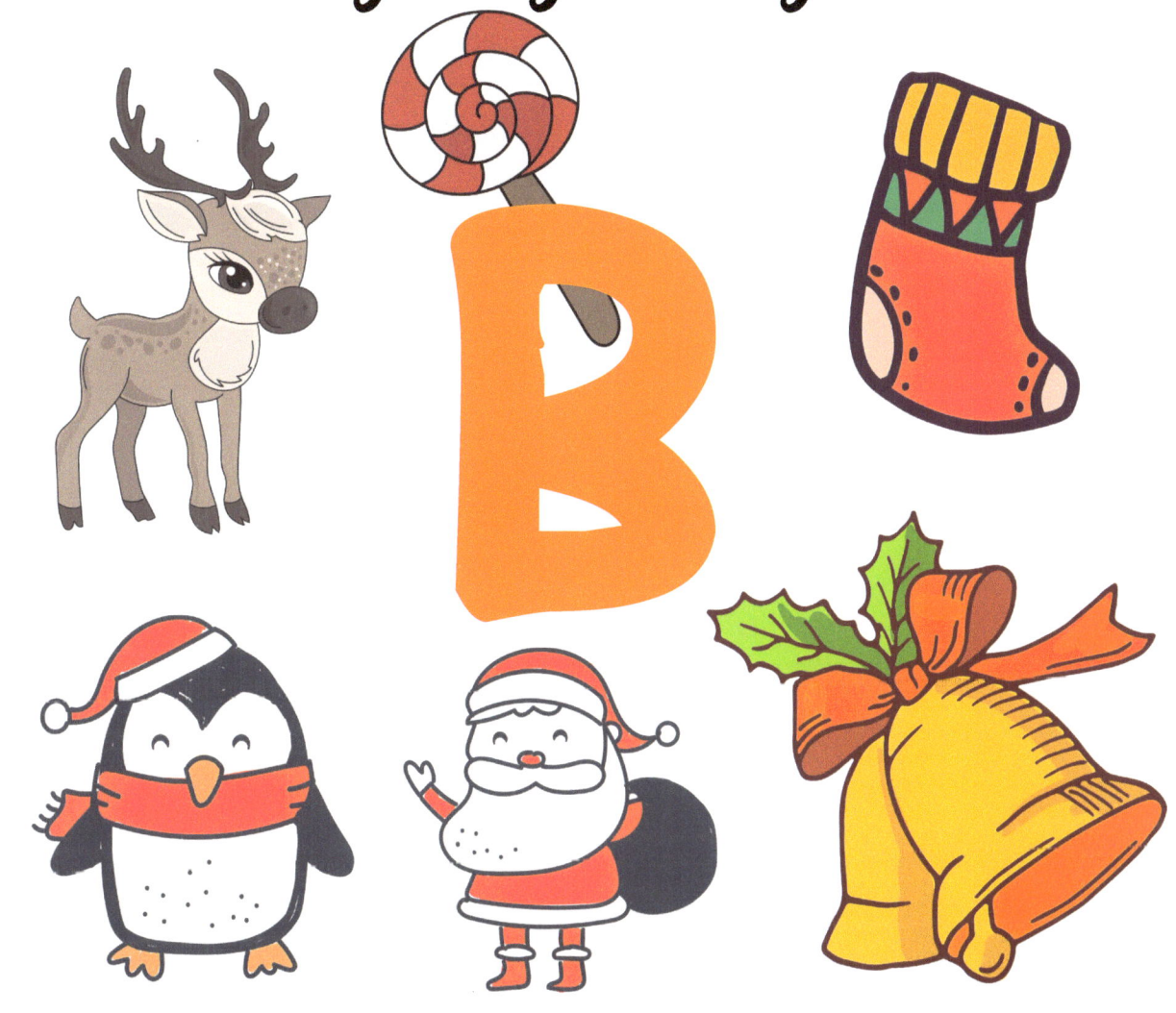

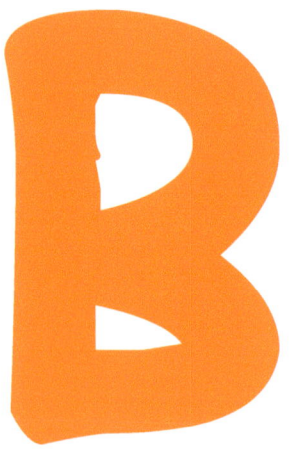

is for bell

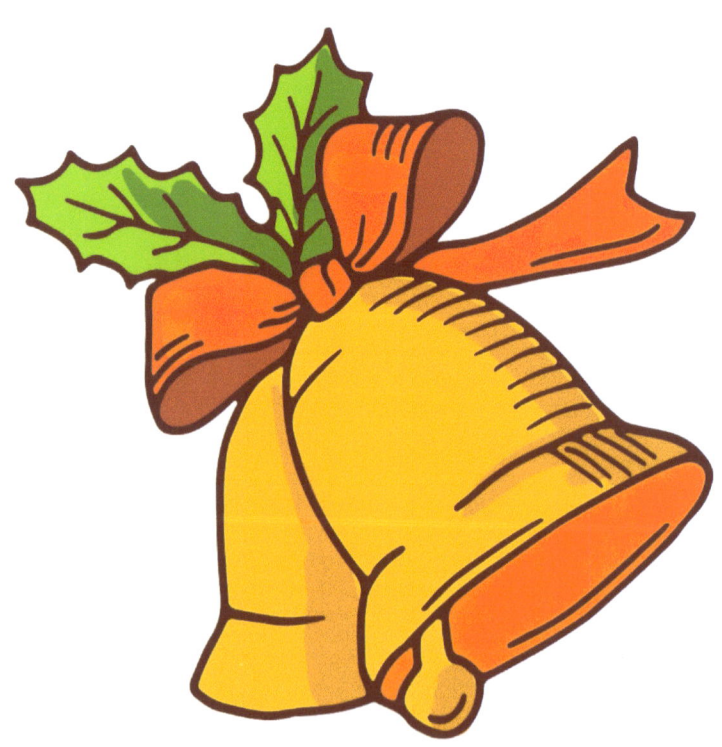

I SPY WITH MY LITTLE EYE ...
something beginning with ...

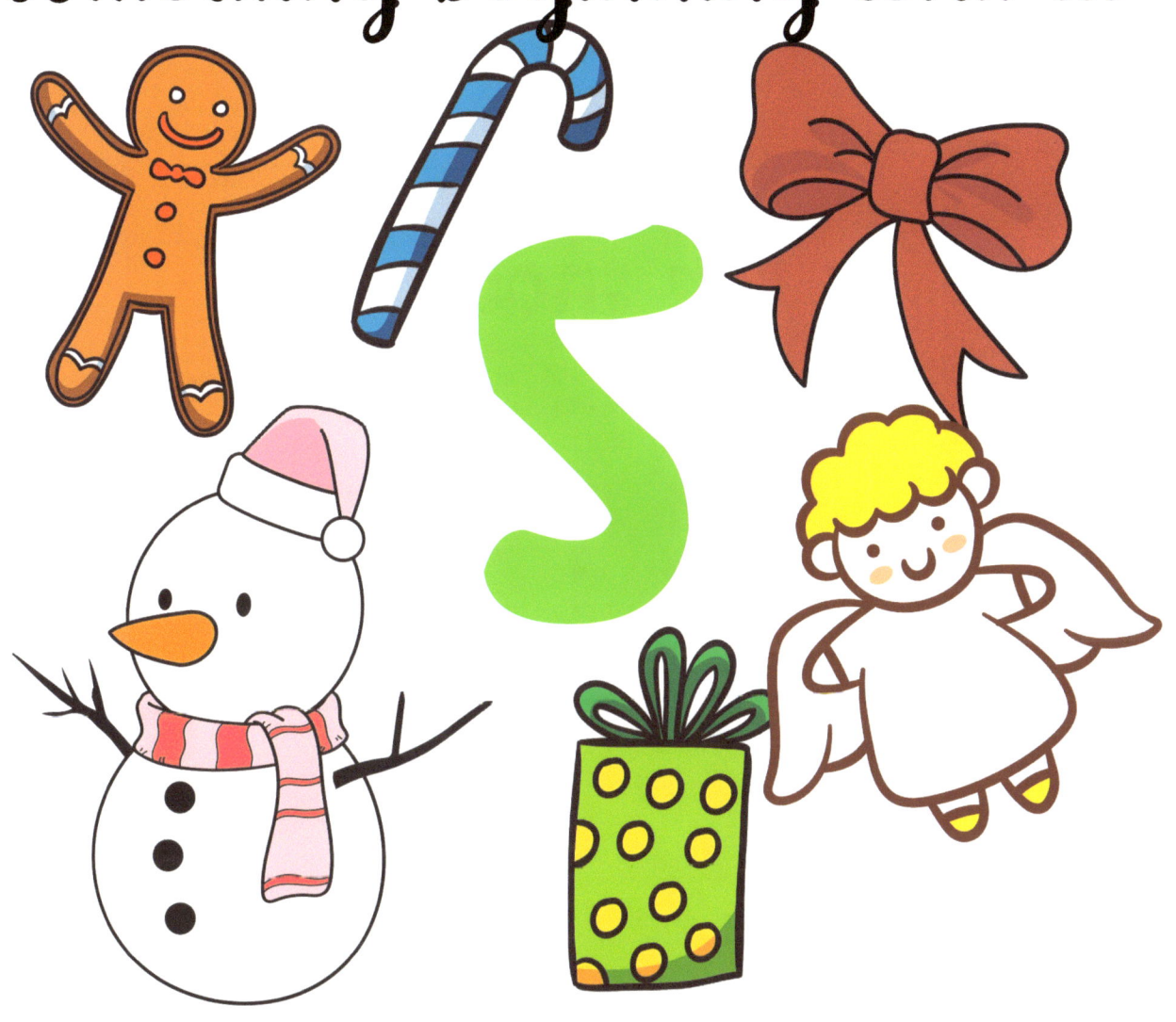

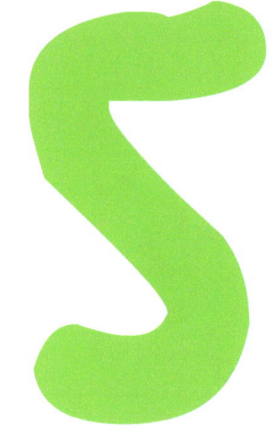

is for snowman

I SPY WITH MY LITTLE EYE ...
something beginning with ...

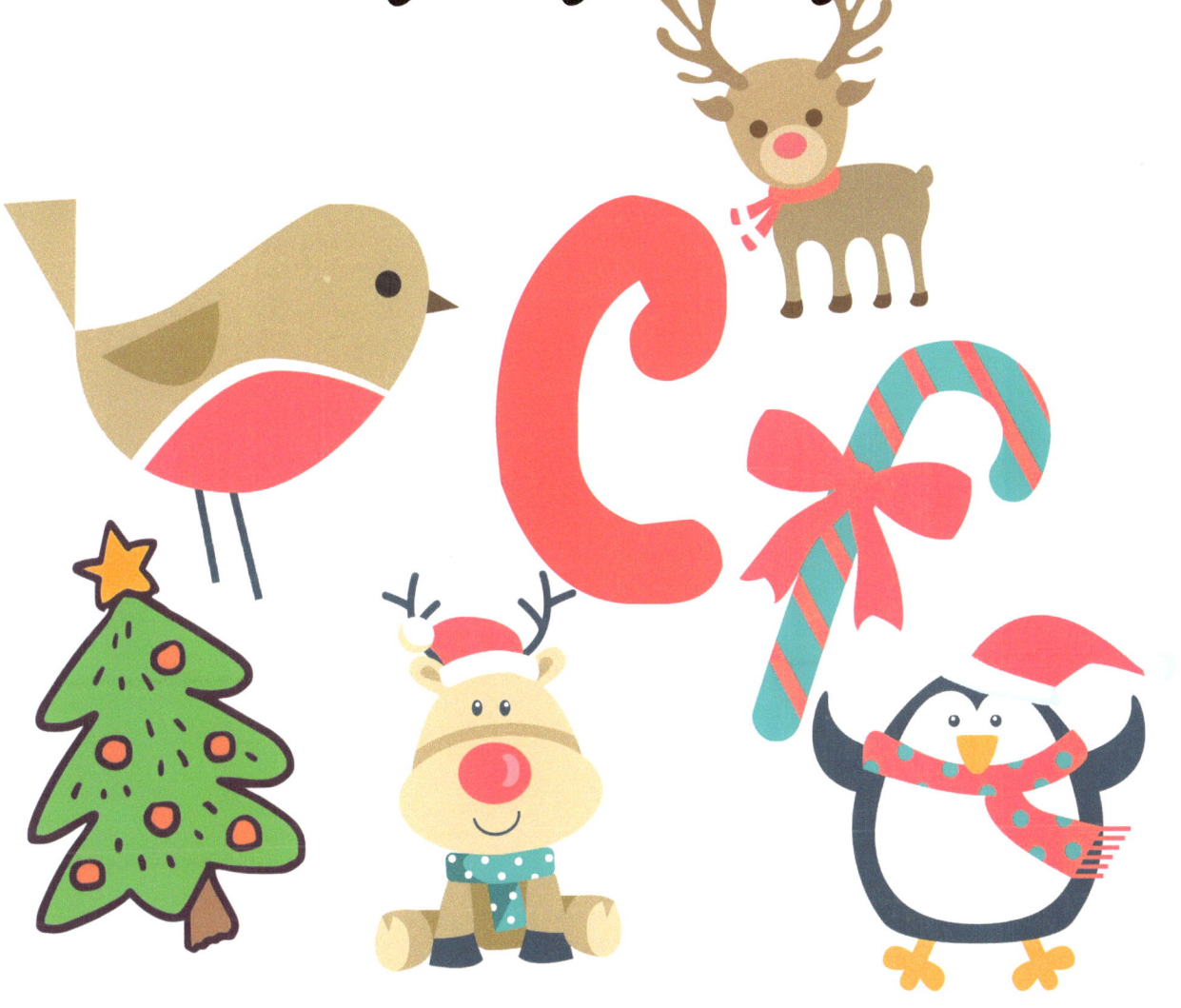

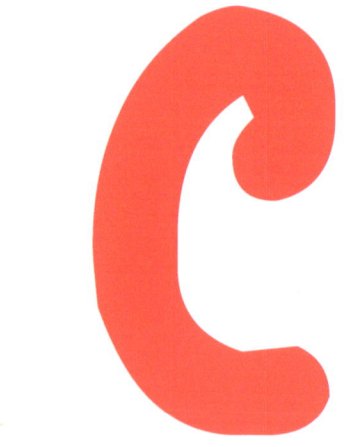

is for candy cane

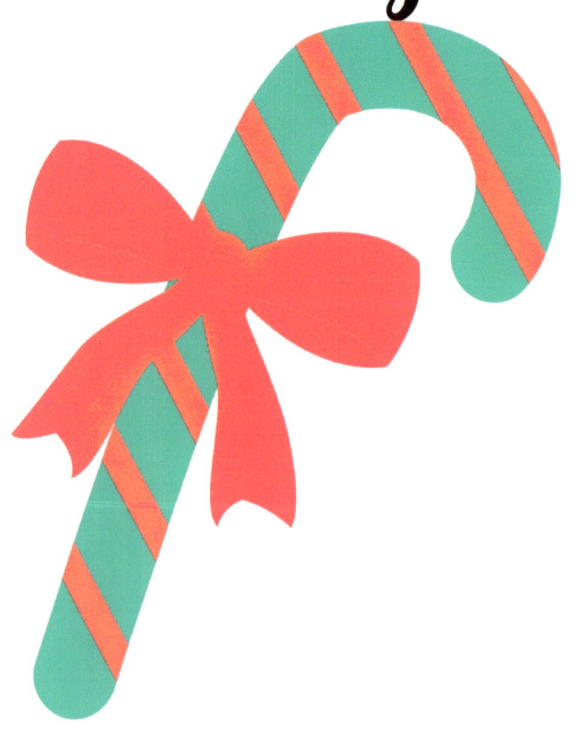

I SPY WITH MY LITTLE EYE ...
something beginning with ...

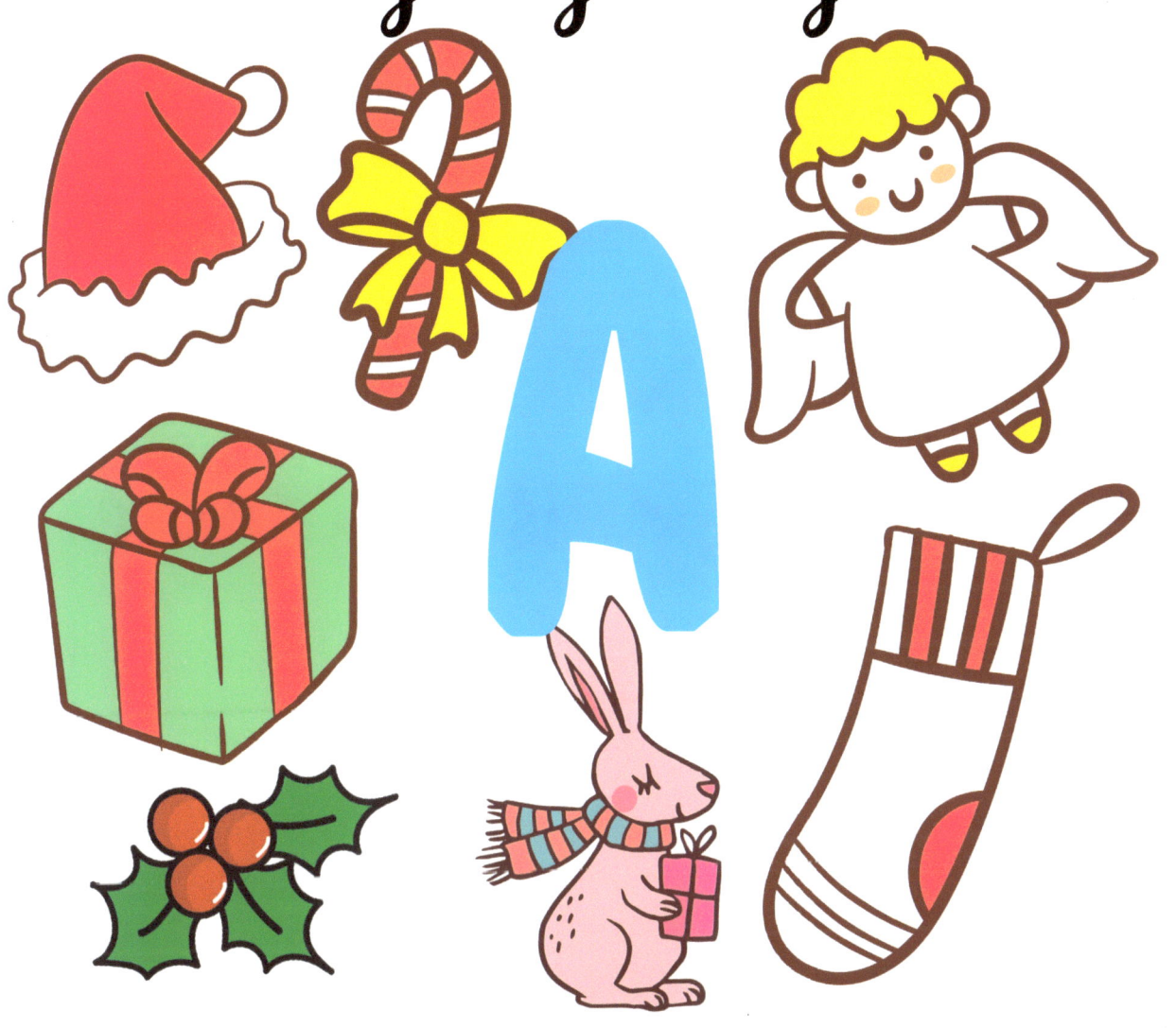

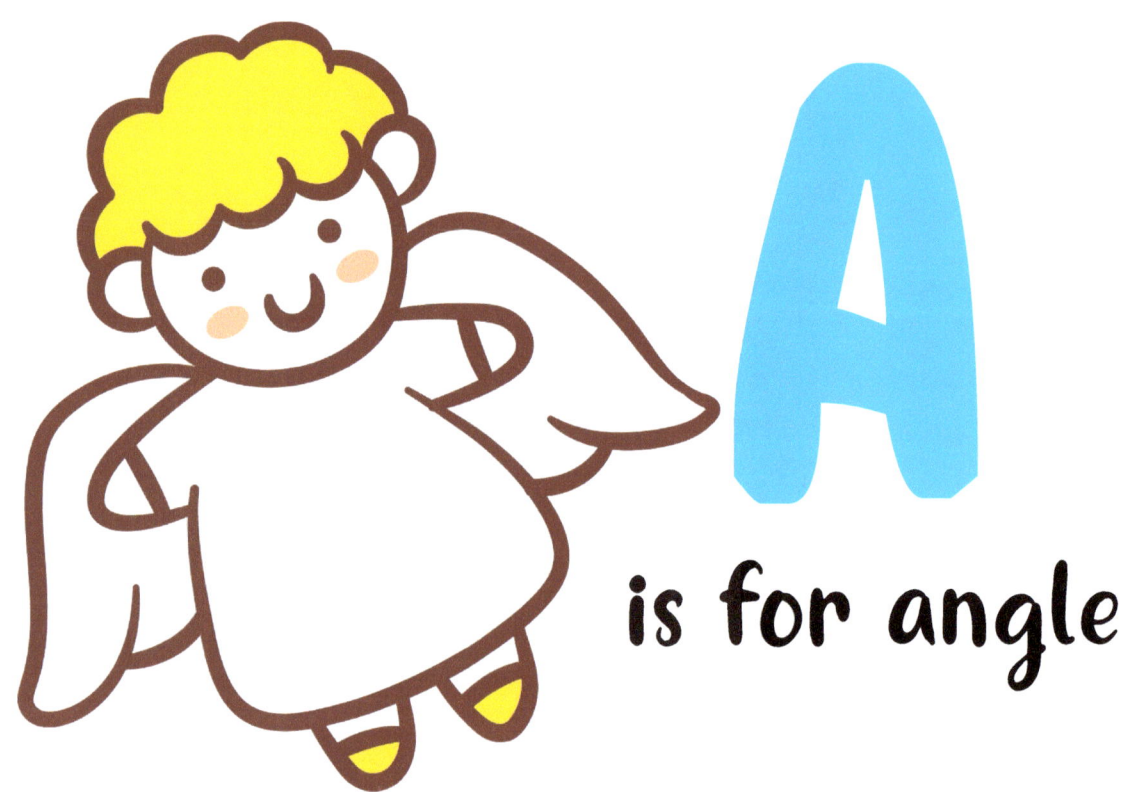

A is for angle

I SPY WITH MY LITTLE EYE ...
something beginning with ...

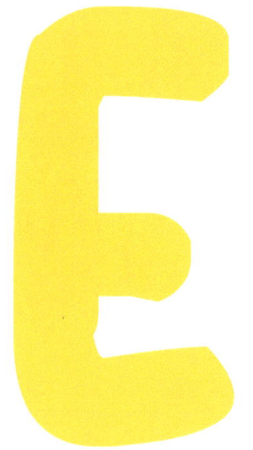

is for elf

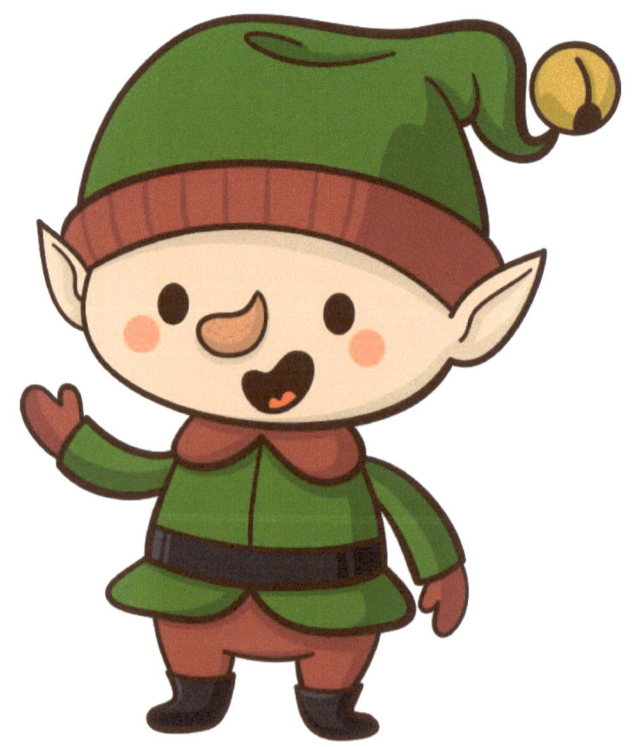

I SPY WITH MY LITTLE EYE ...
something beginning with ...

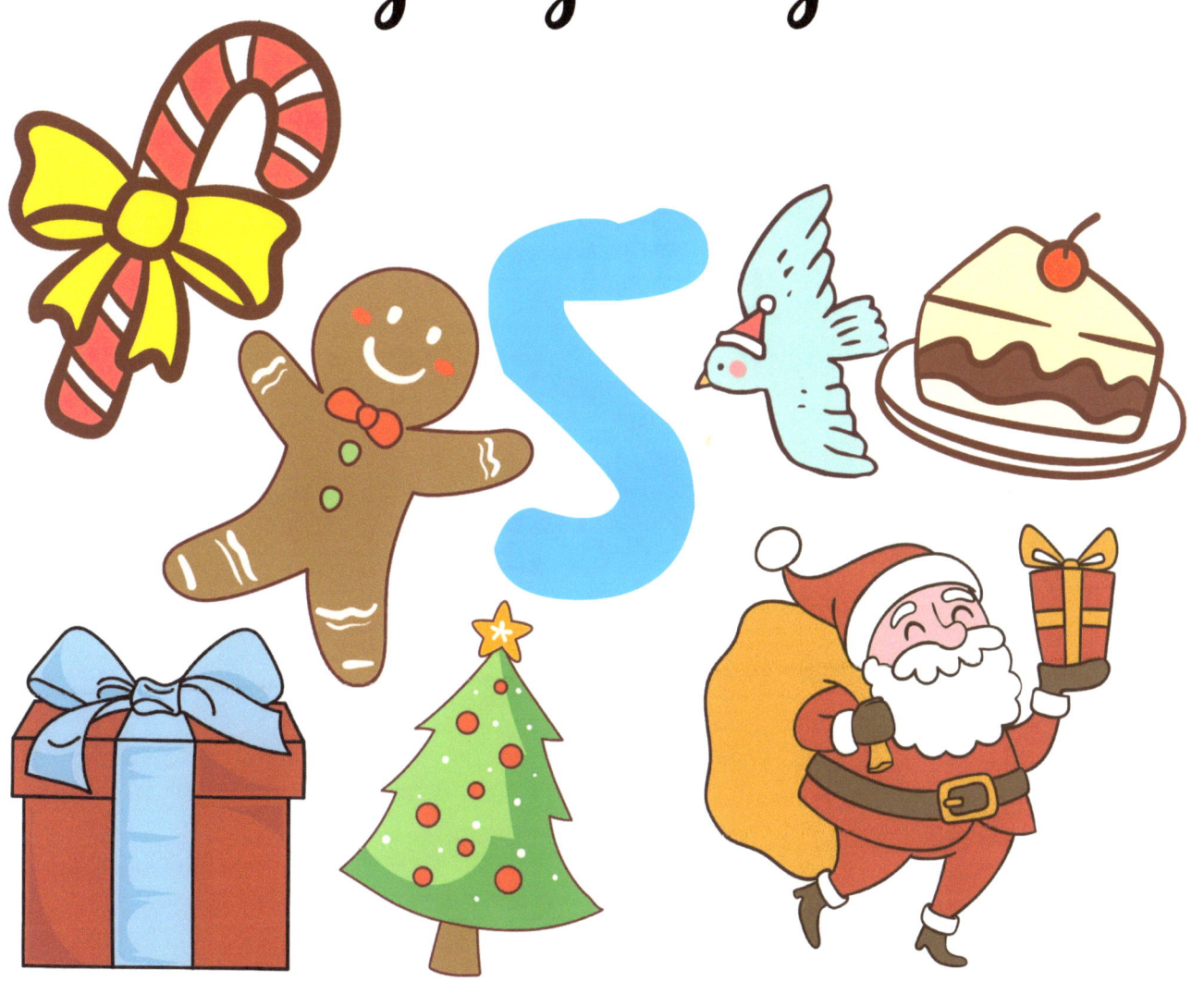

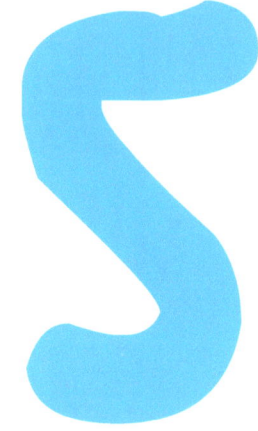

is for santa

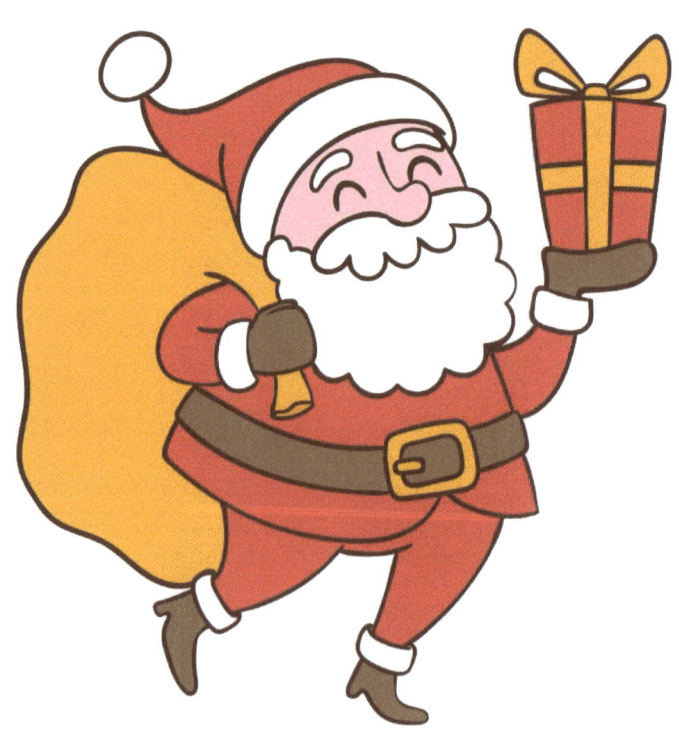

I SPY WITH MY LITTLE EYE ...
something beginning with ...

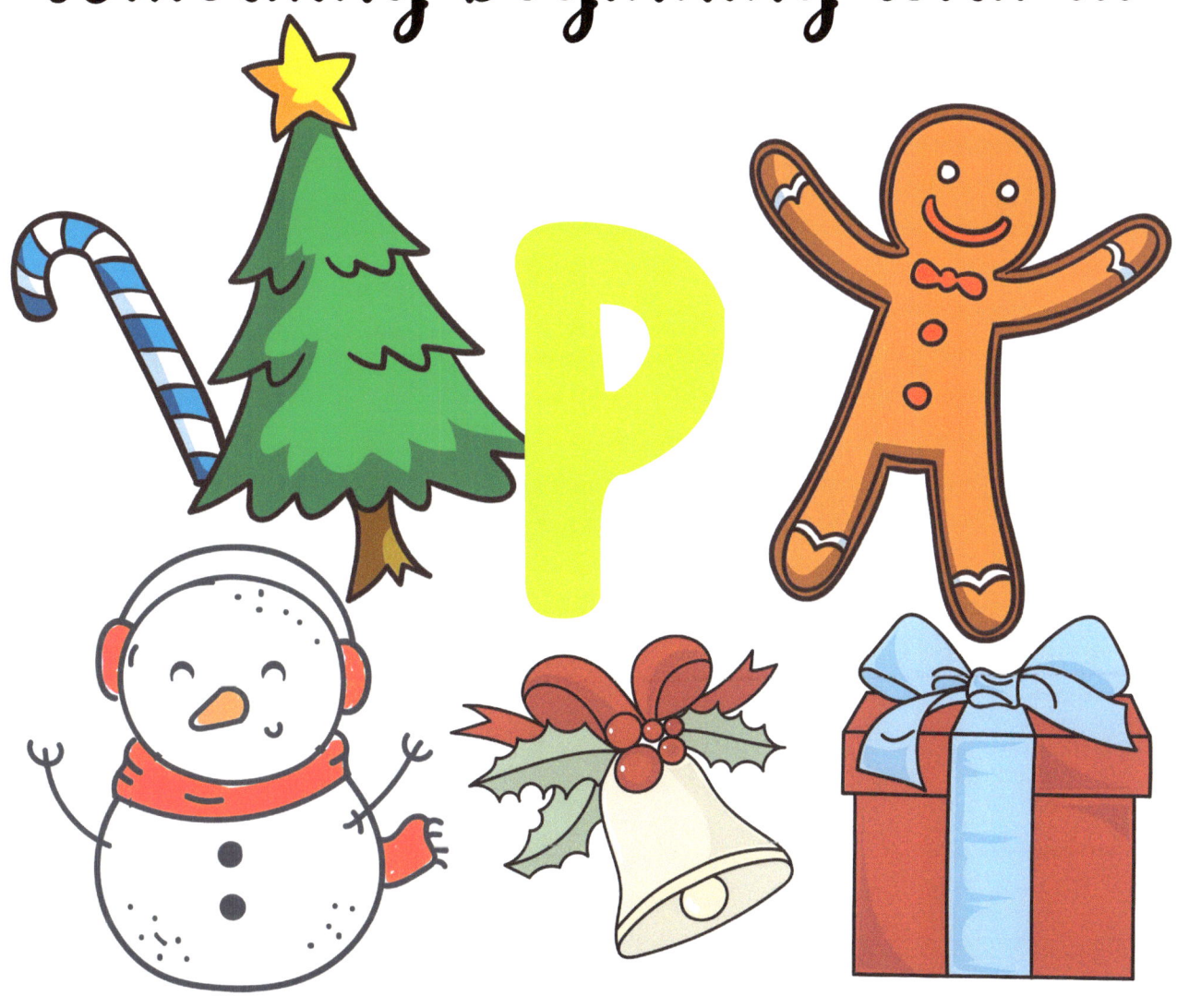

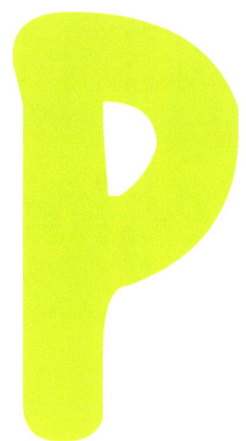

is for present

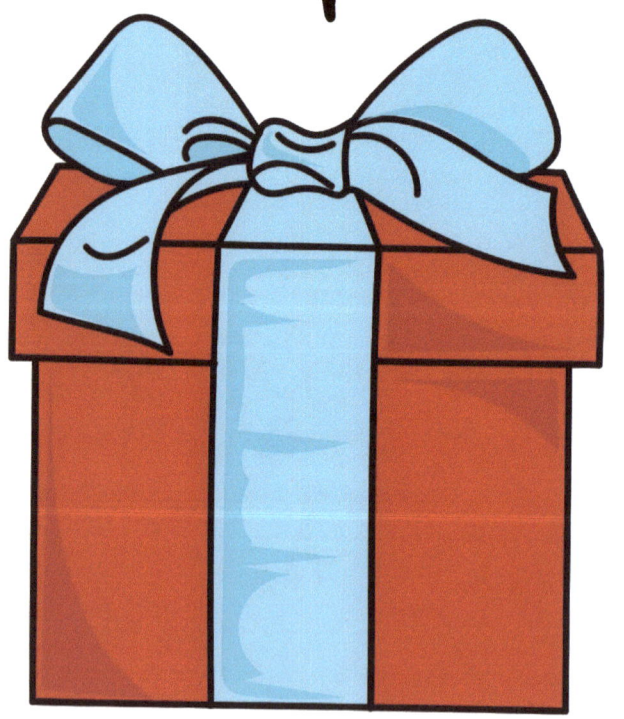

I SPY WITH MY LITTLE EYE ...
something beginning with ...

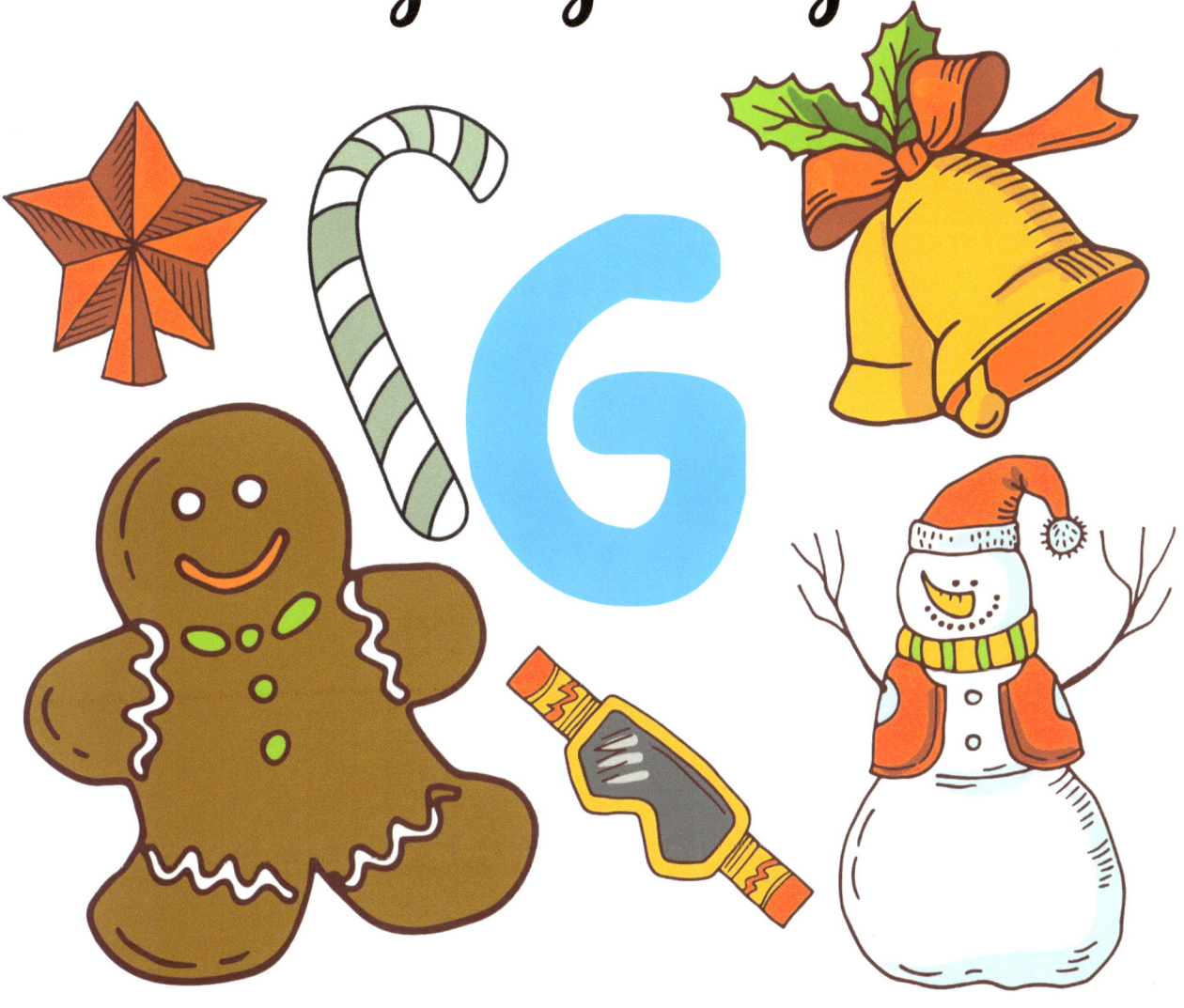

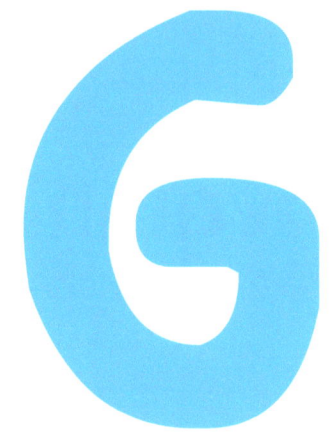

is for gingerbread

I SPY WITH MY LITTLE EYE ...
something beginning with ...

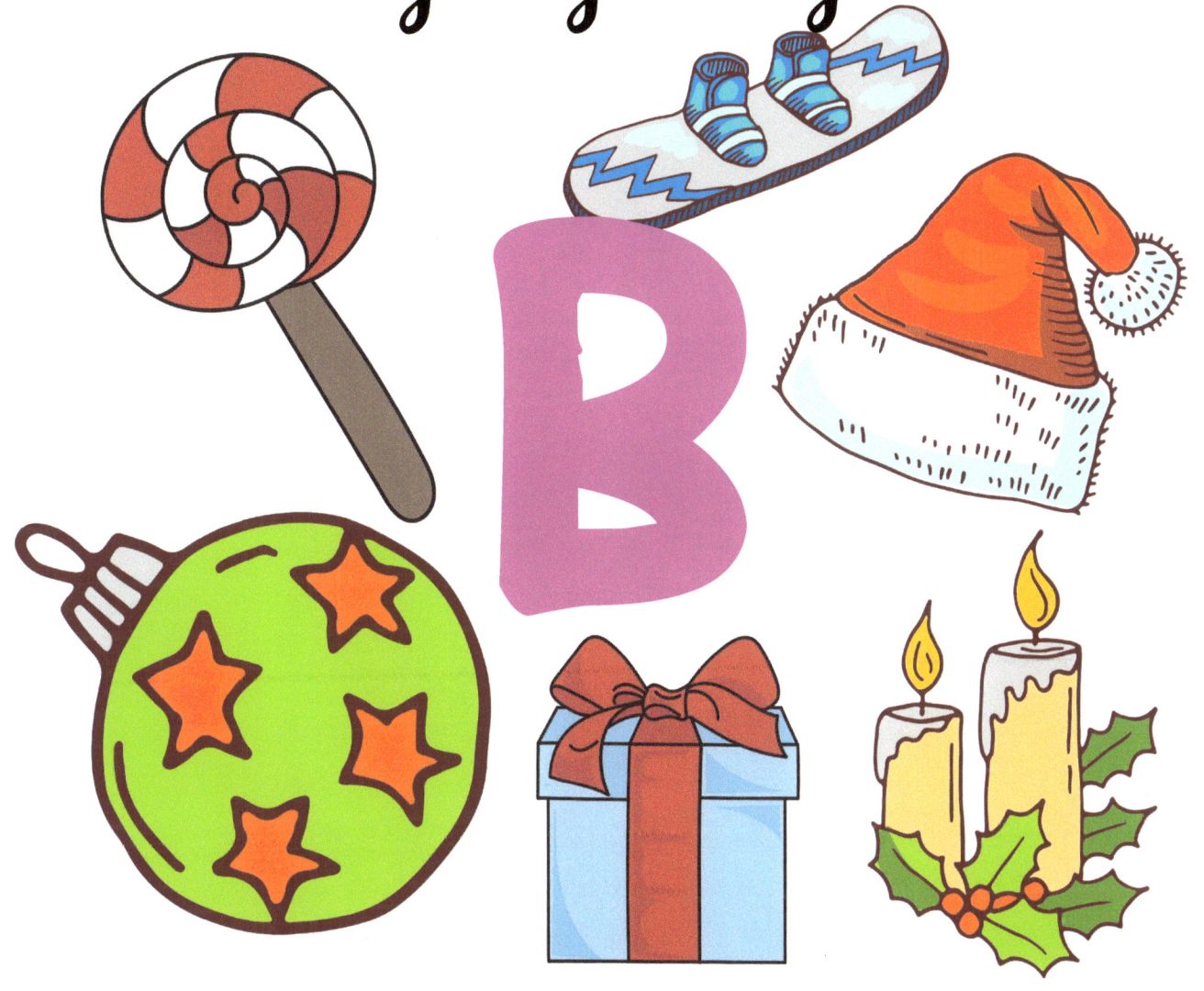

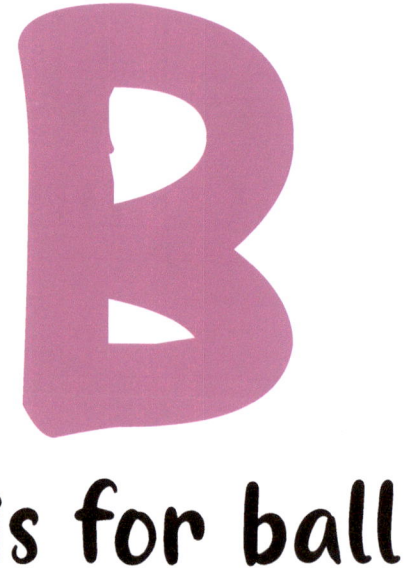

is for ball

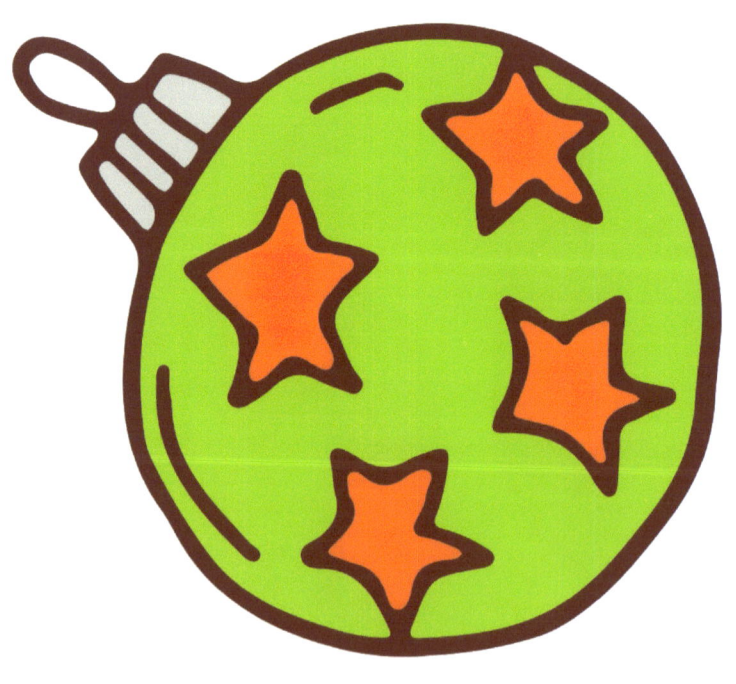

I SPY WITH MY LITTLE EYE ...
something beginning with ...

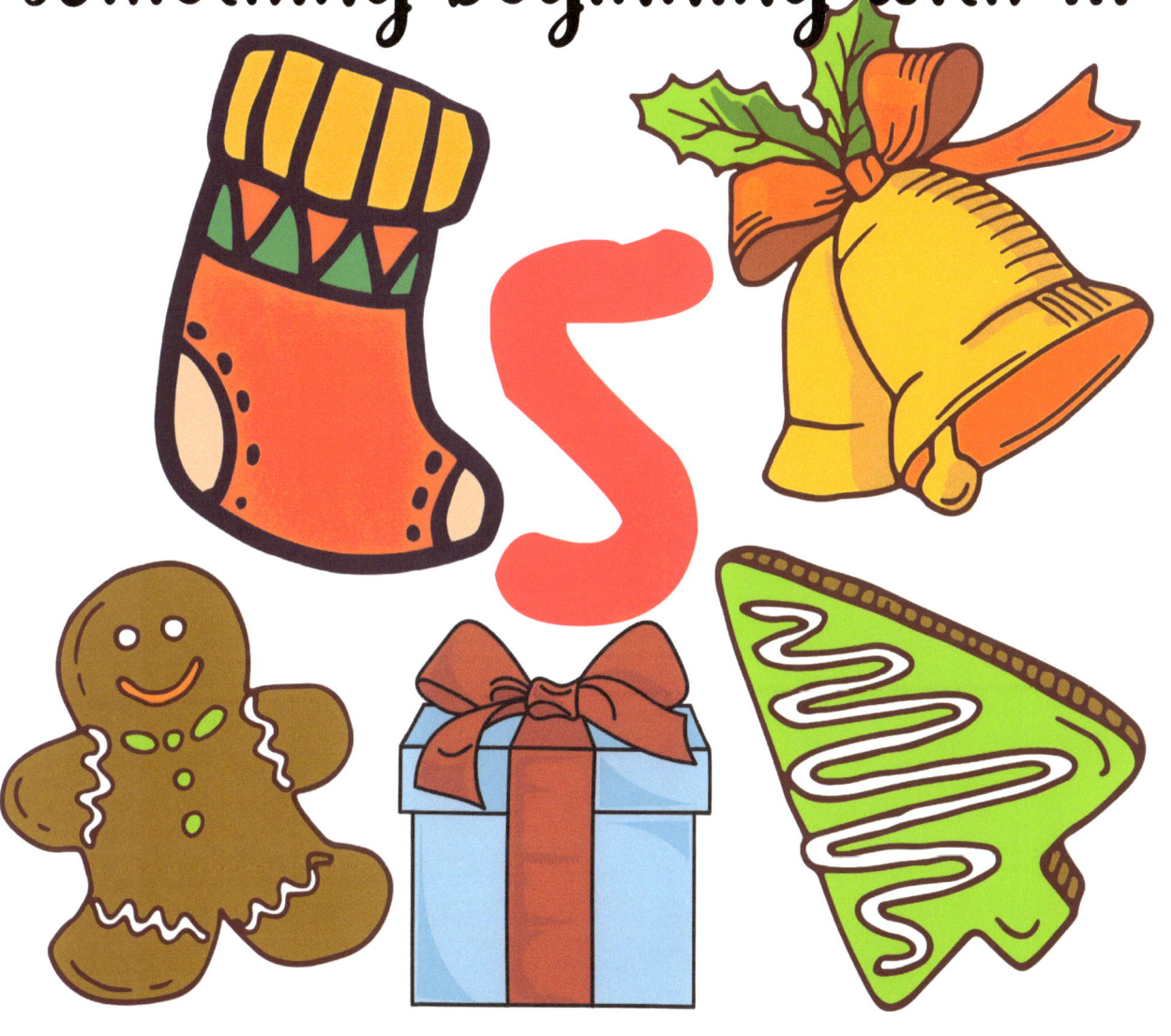

S

is for stocking

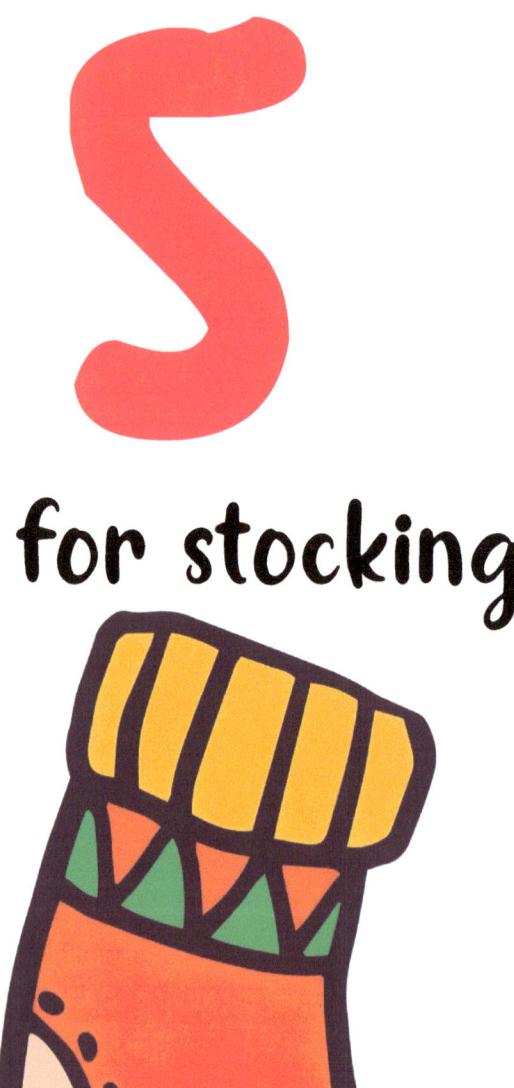

I SPY WITH MY LITTLE EYE ...
something beginning with ...

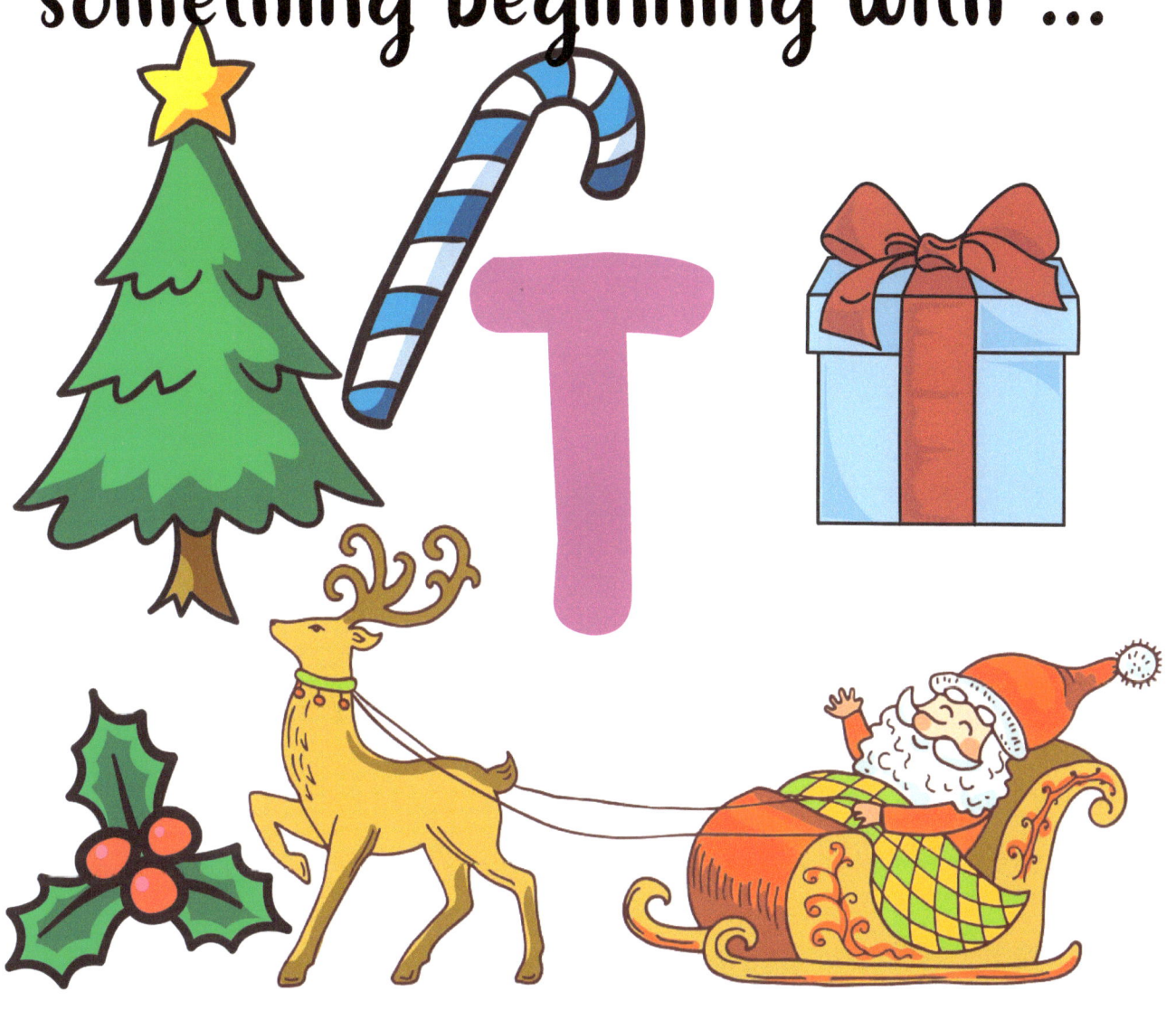

T is for tree

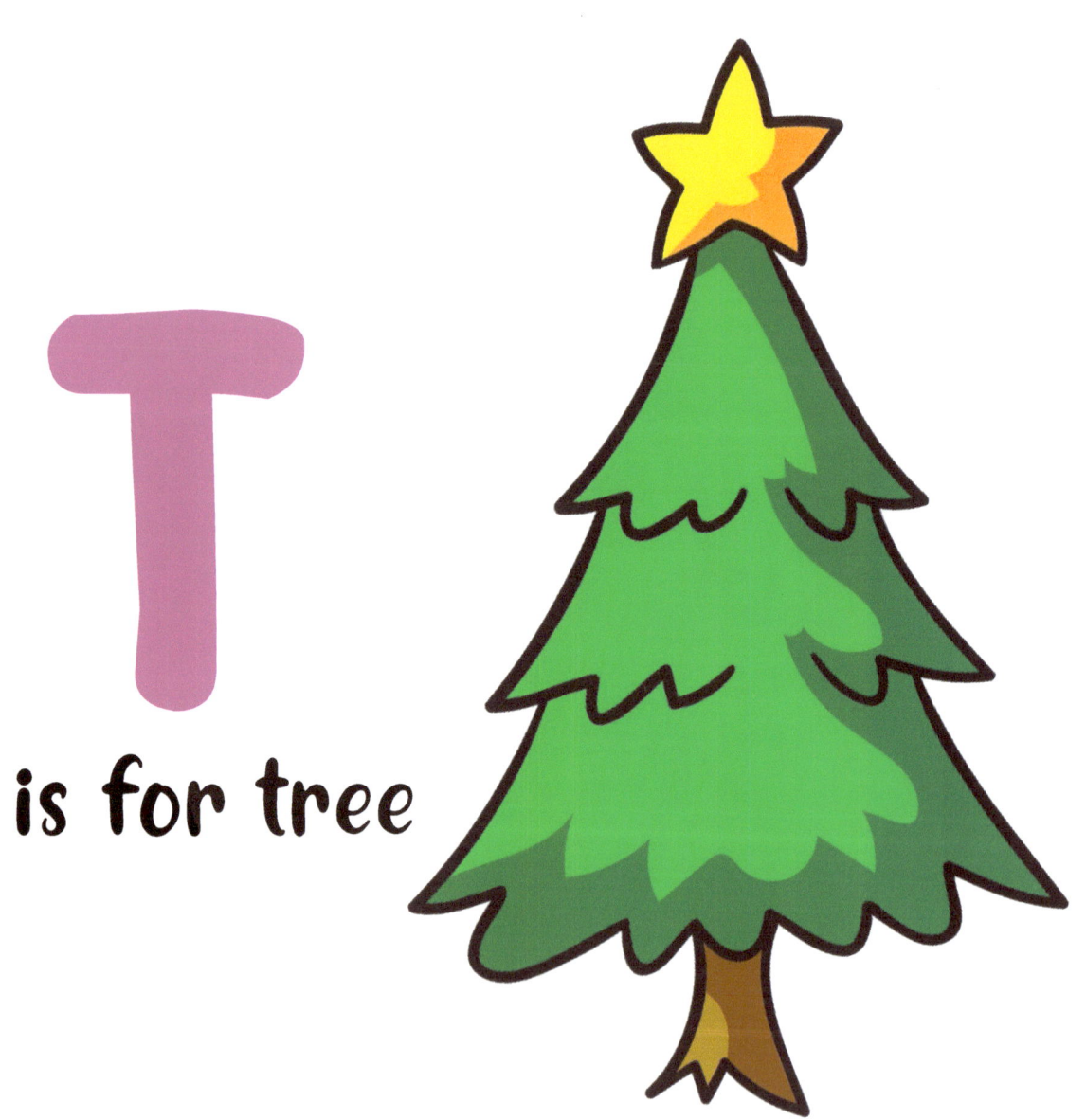

I SPY WITH MY LITTLE EYE ...
something beginning with ...

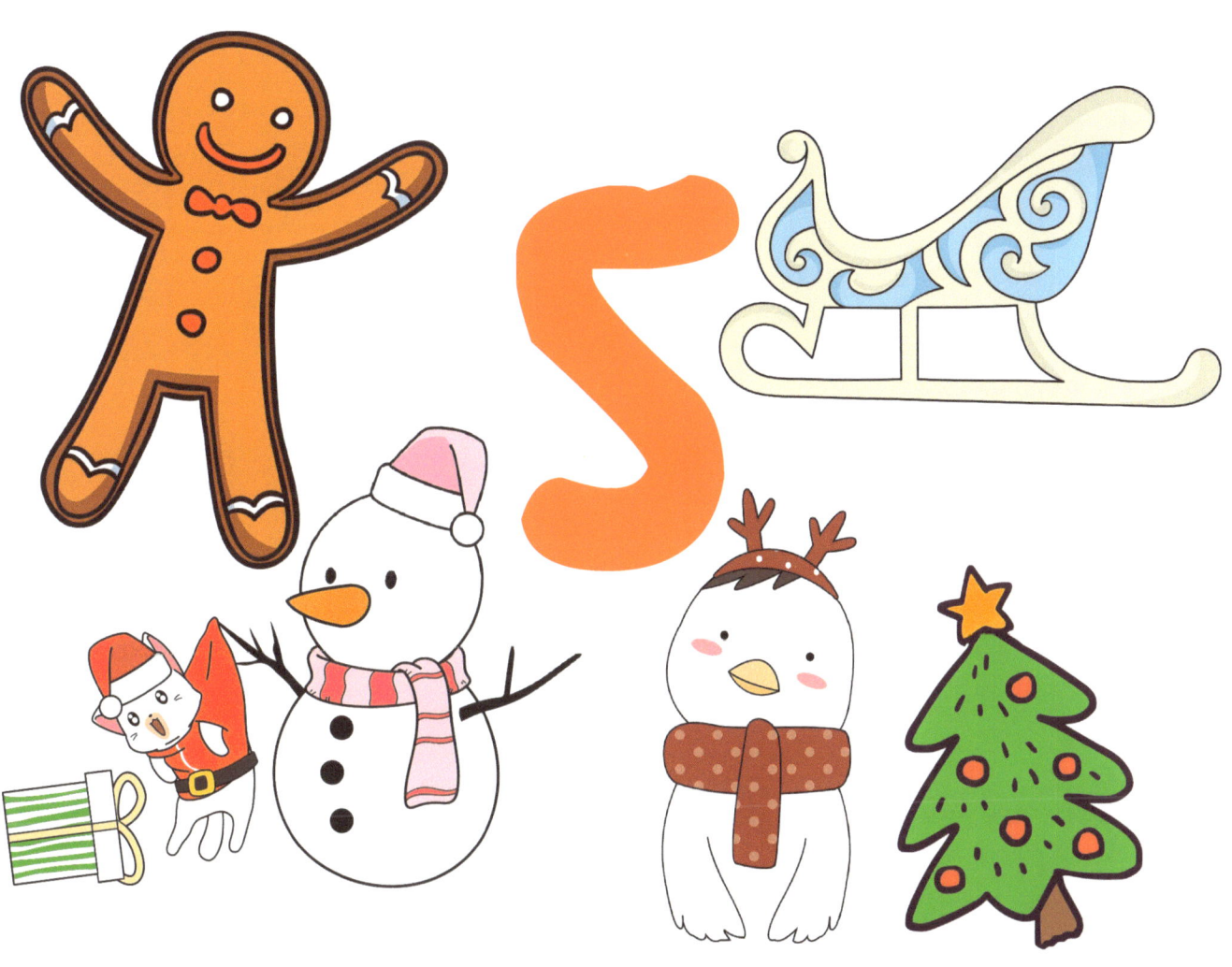

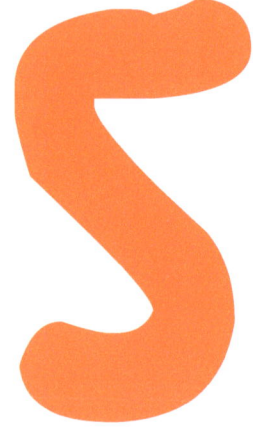

is for sleigh

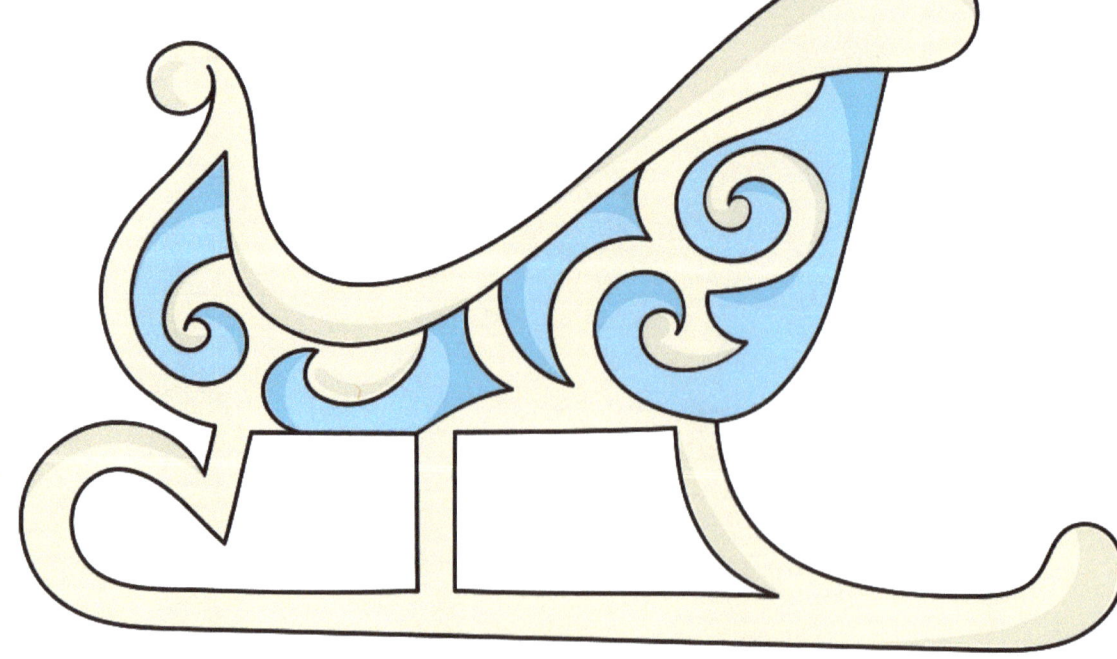

I SPY WITH MY LITTLE EYE ...
something beginning with ...

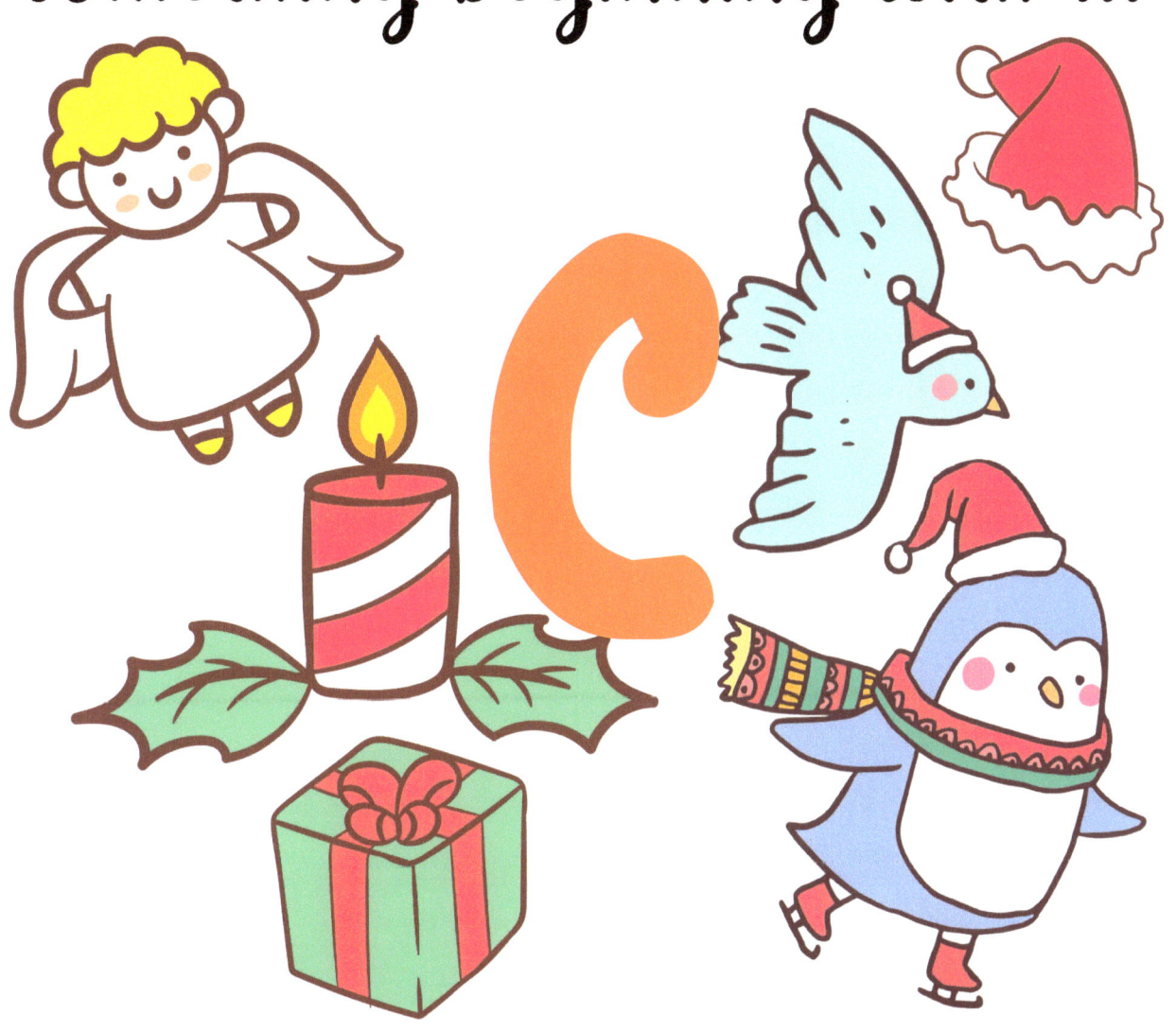

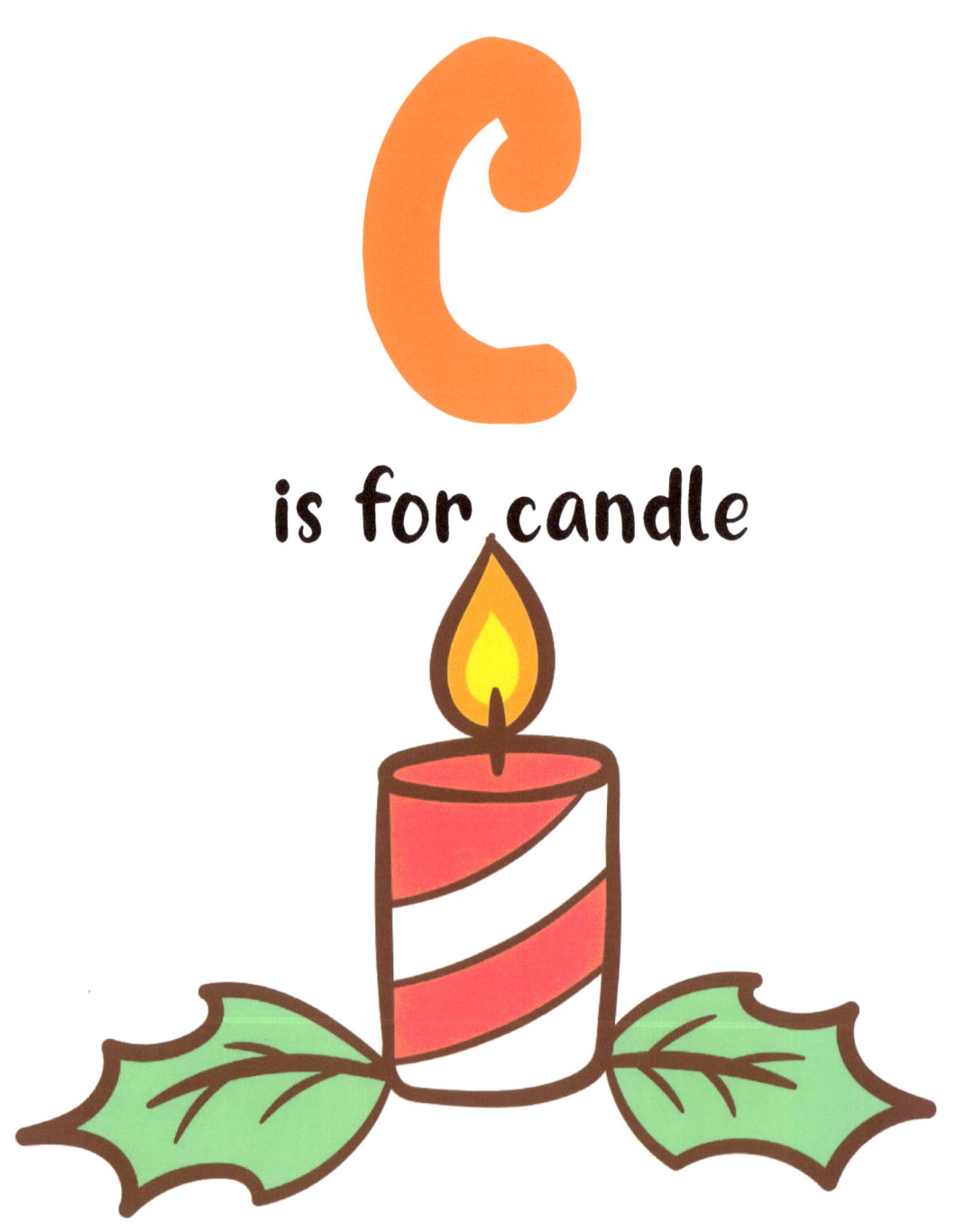

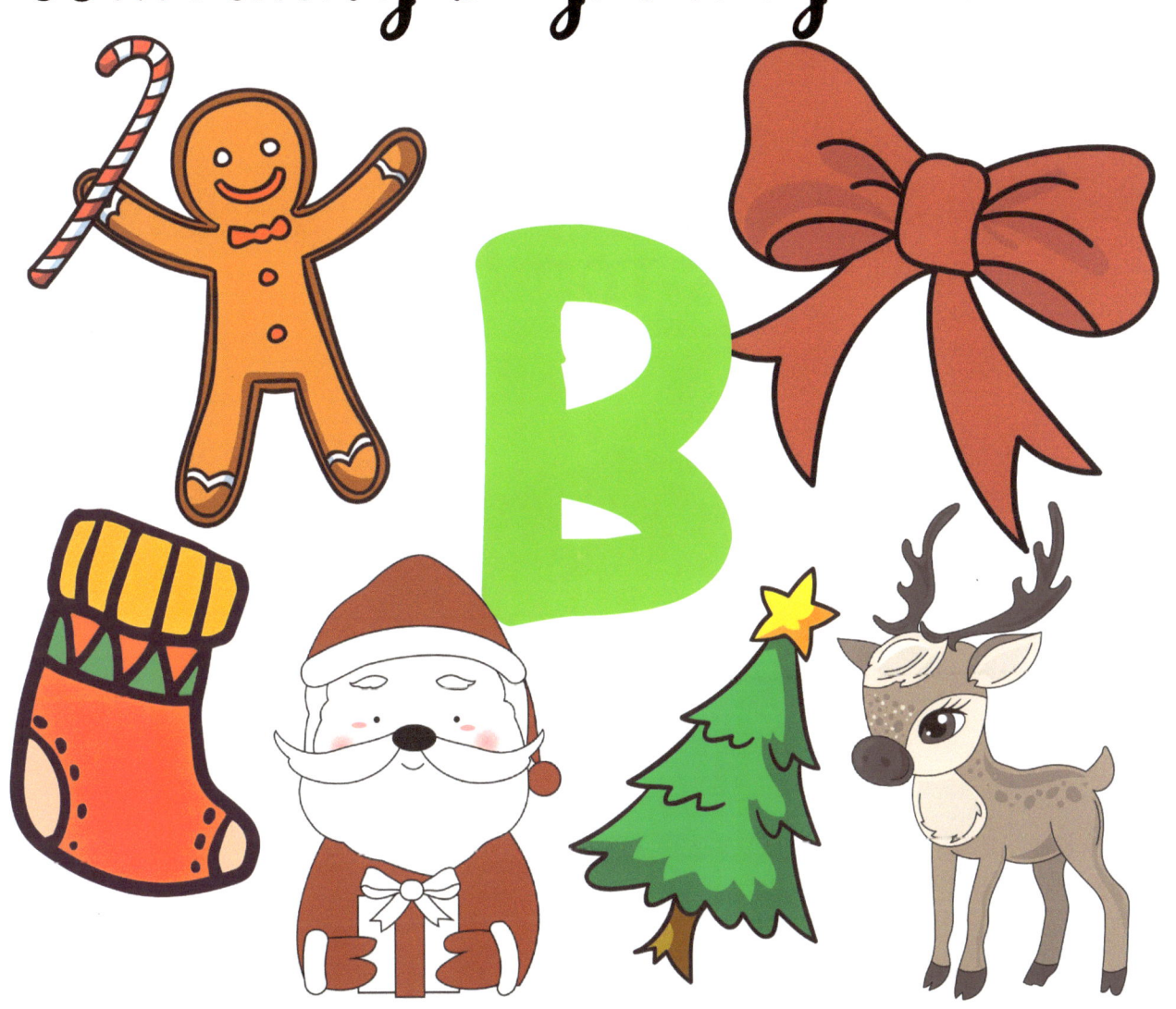

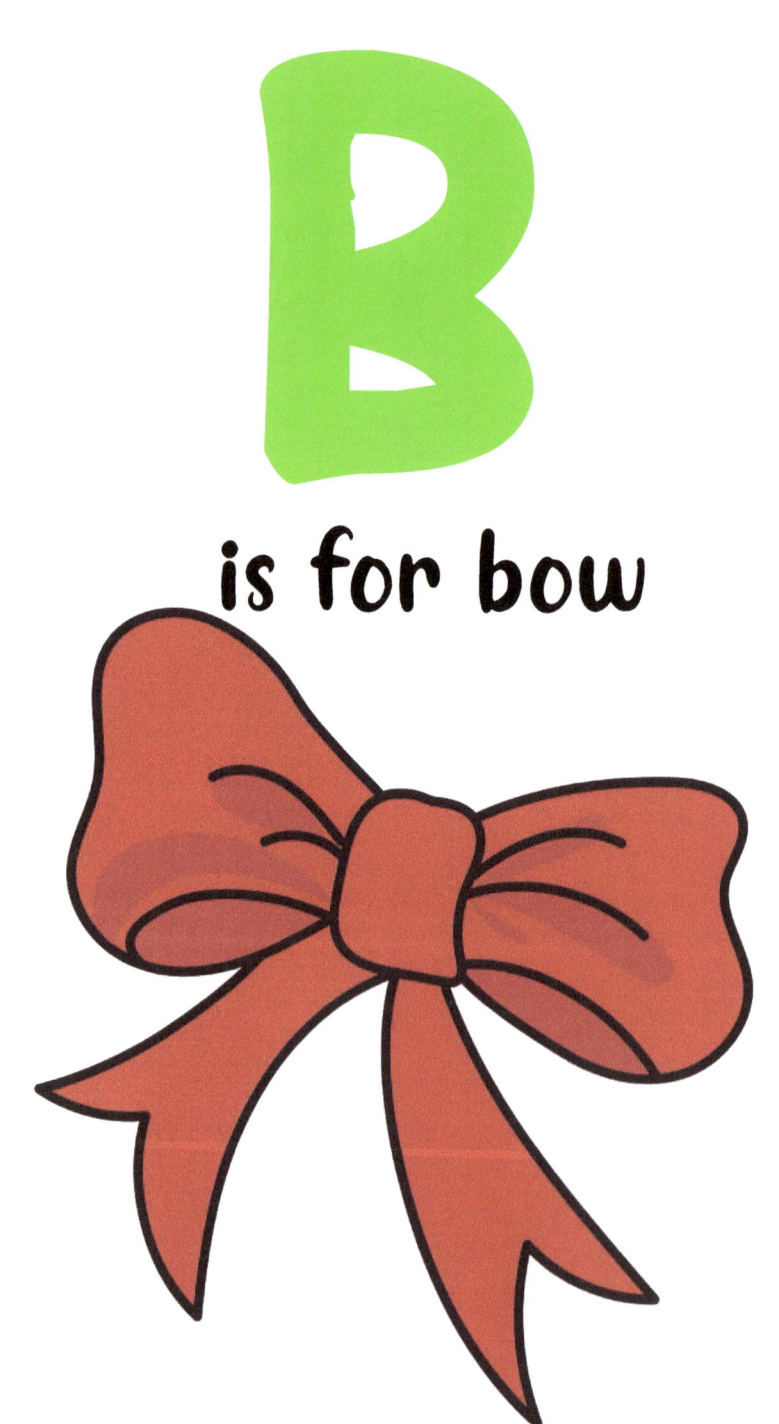
B
is for bow

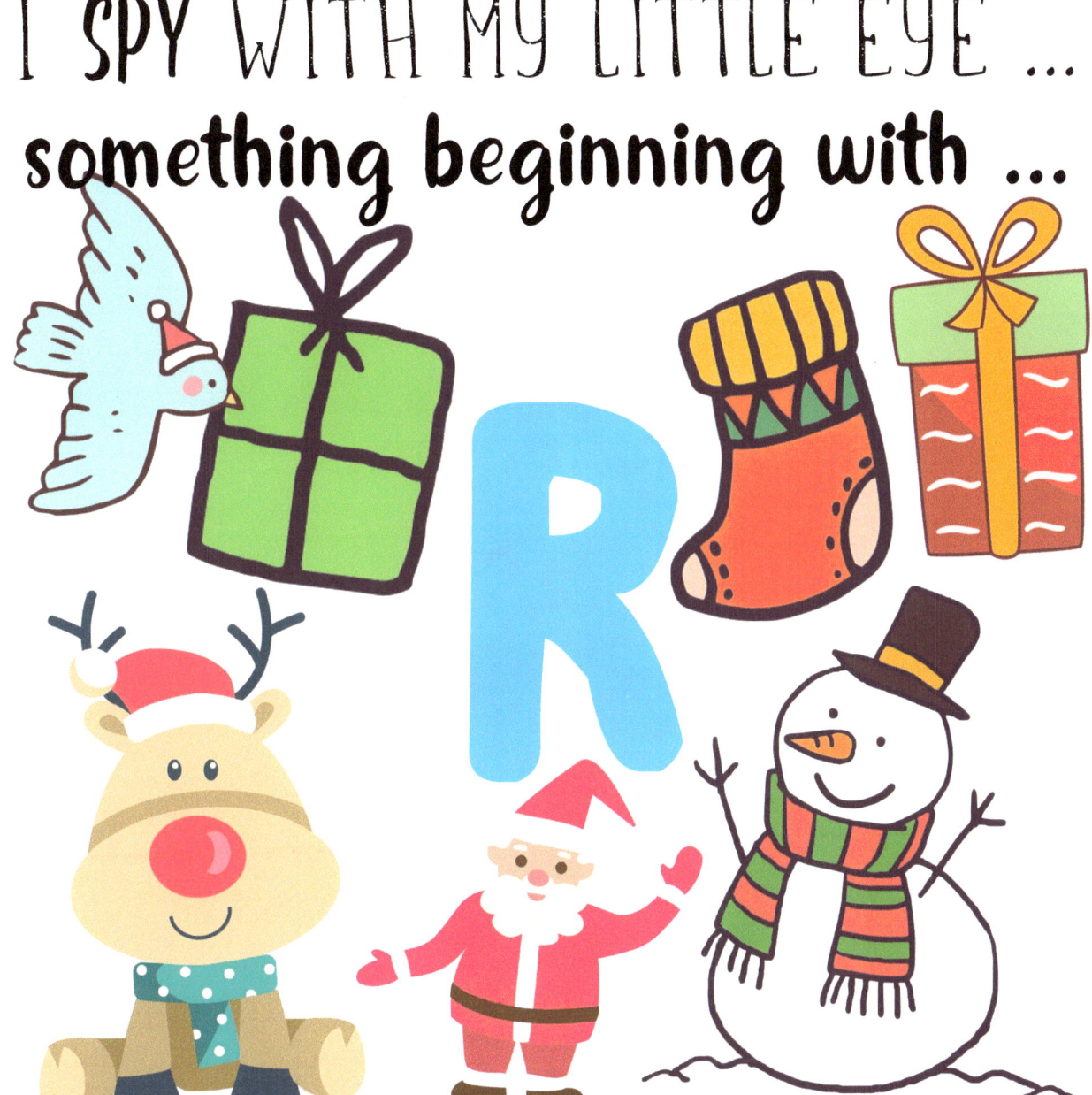

R
is for reindeer

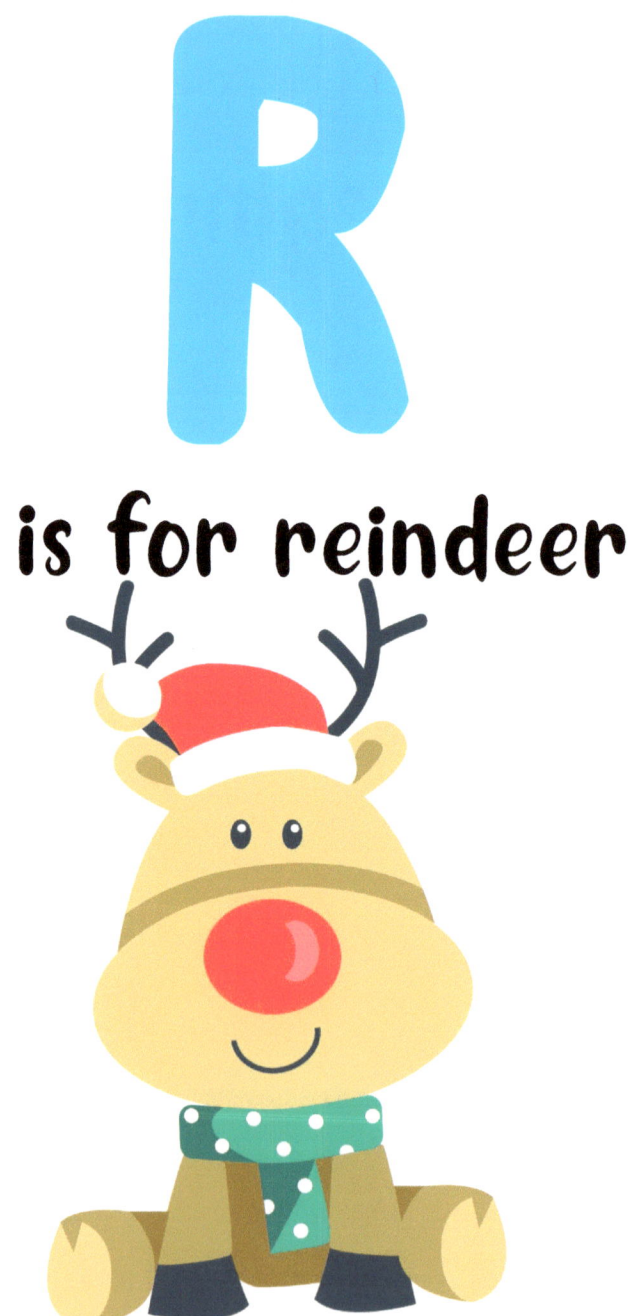

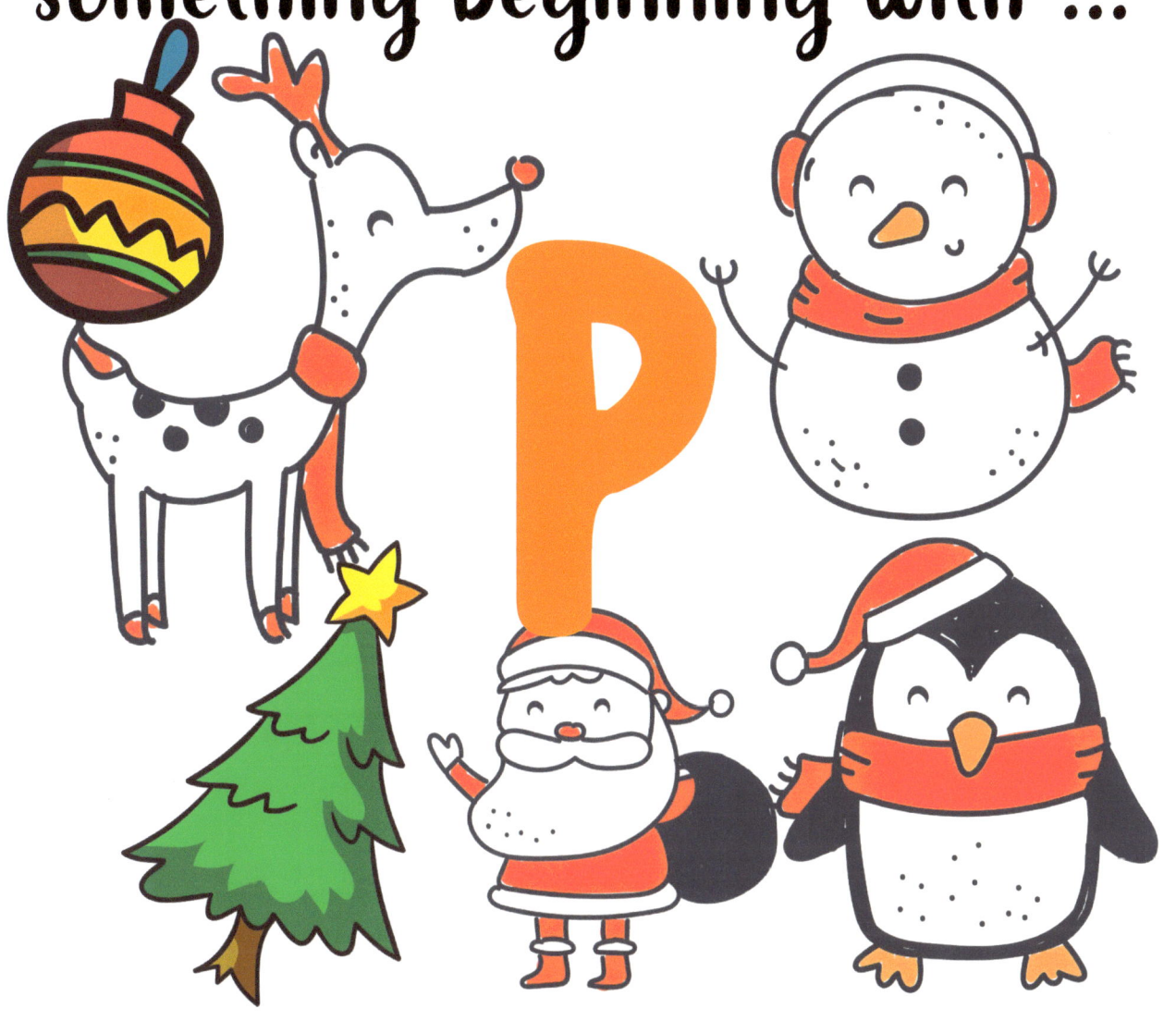

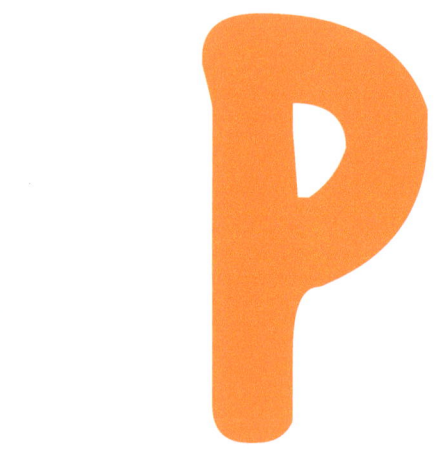

is for penguine

I SPY WITH MY LITTLE EYE ...
something beginning with ...

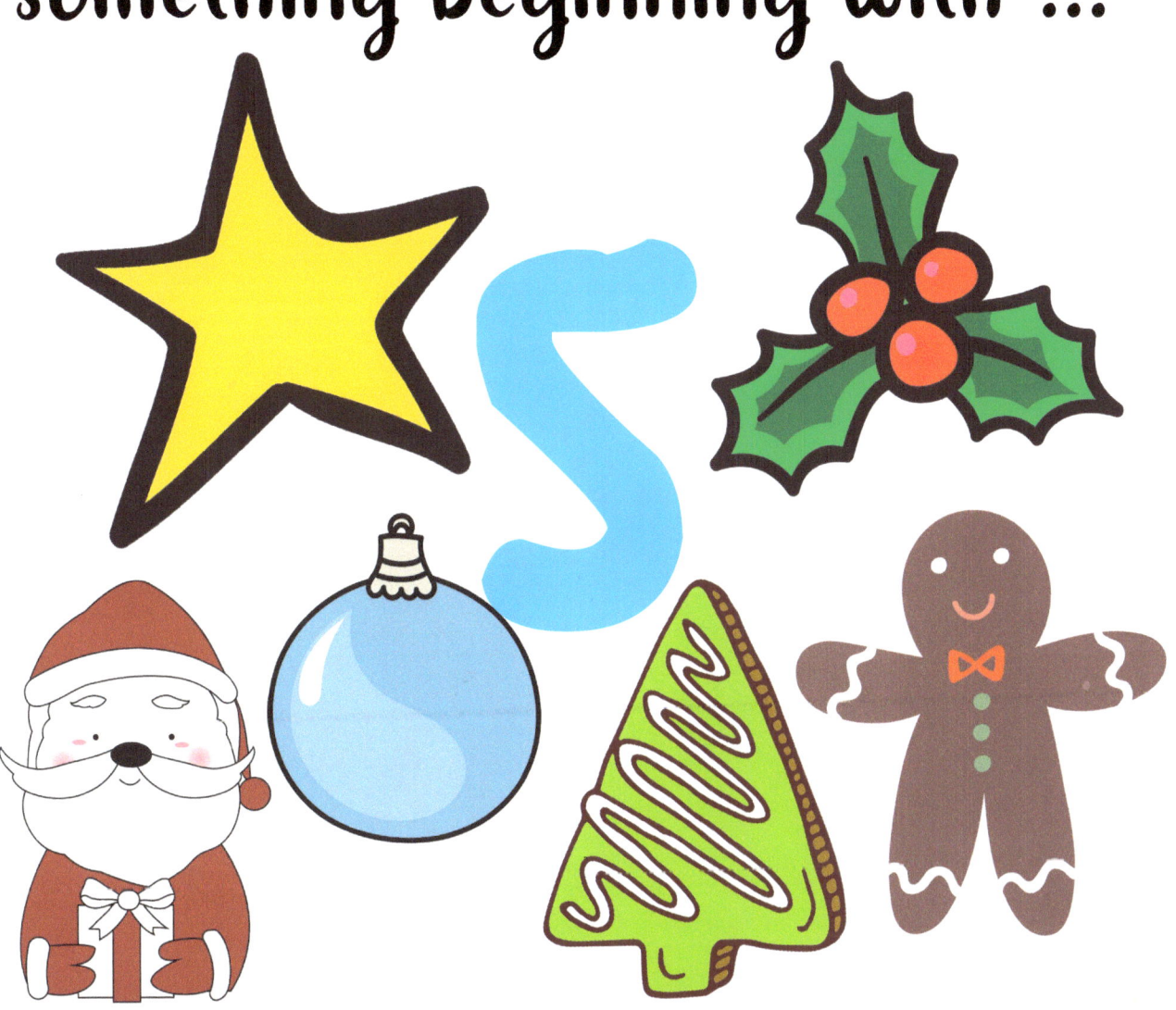

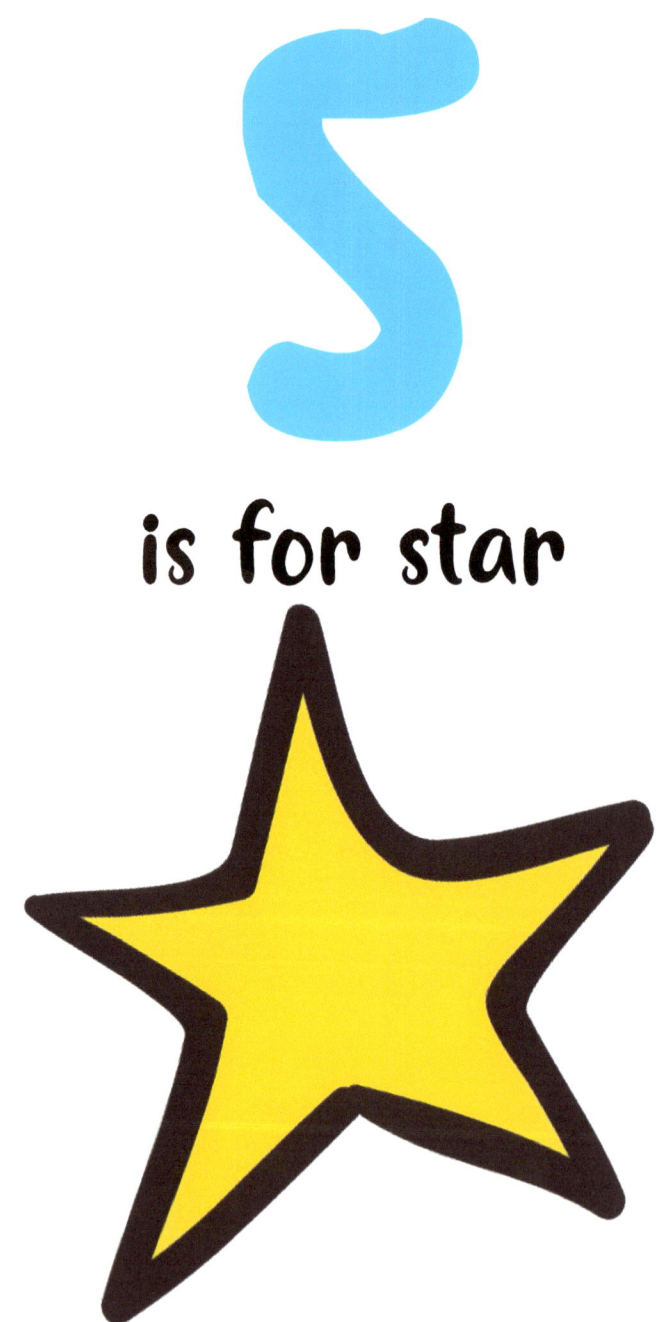

I SPY WITH MY LITTLE EYE ...
something beginning with ...

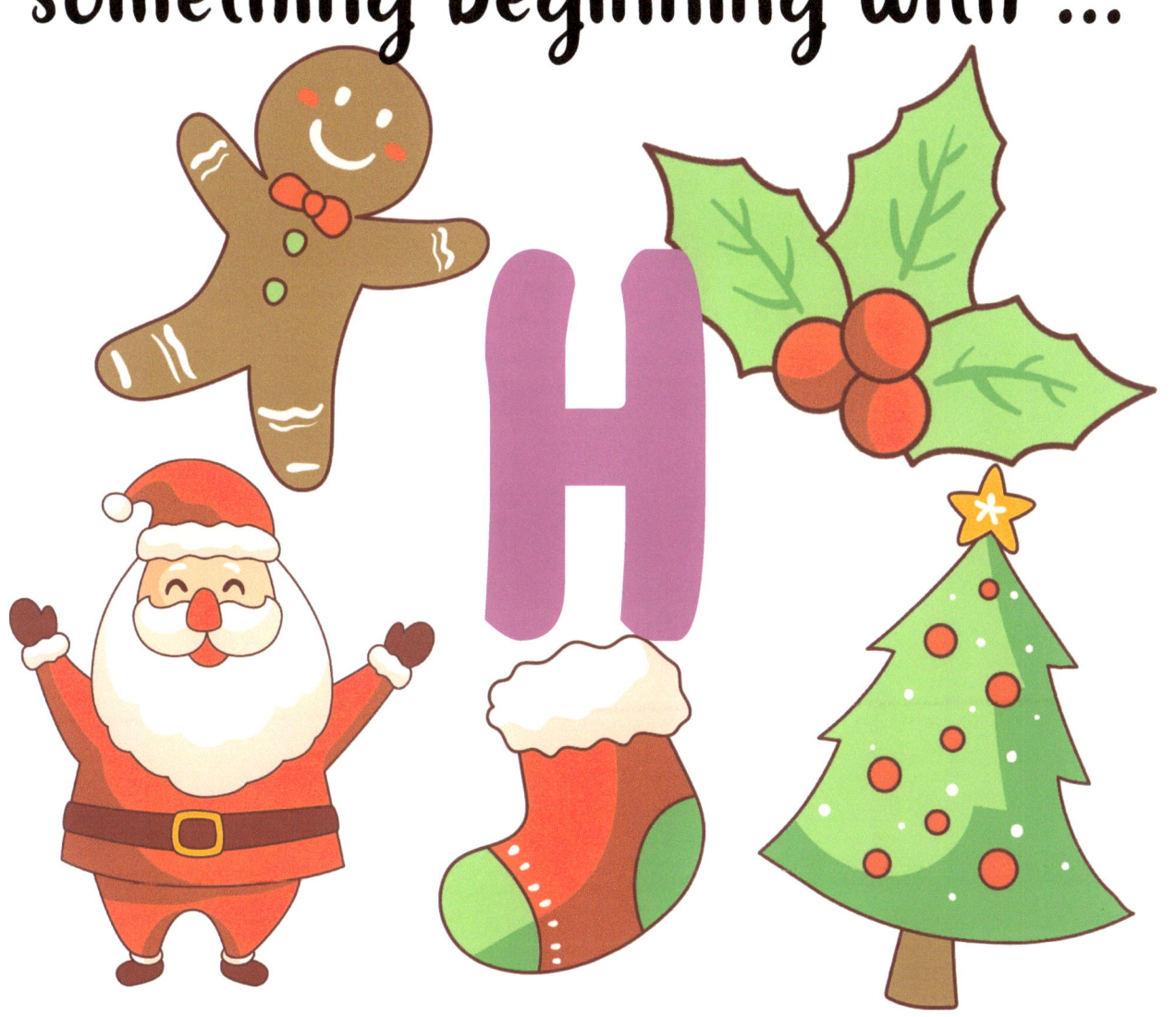

H
is for holly

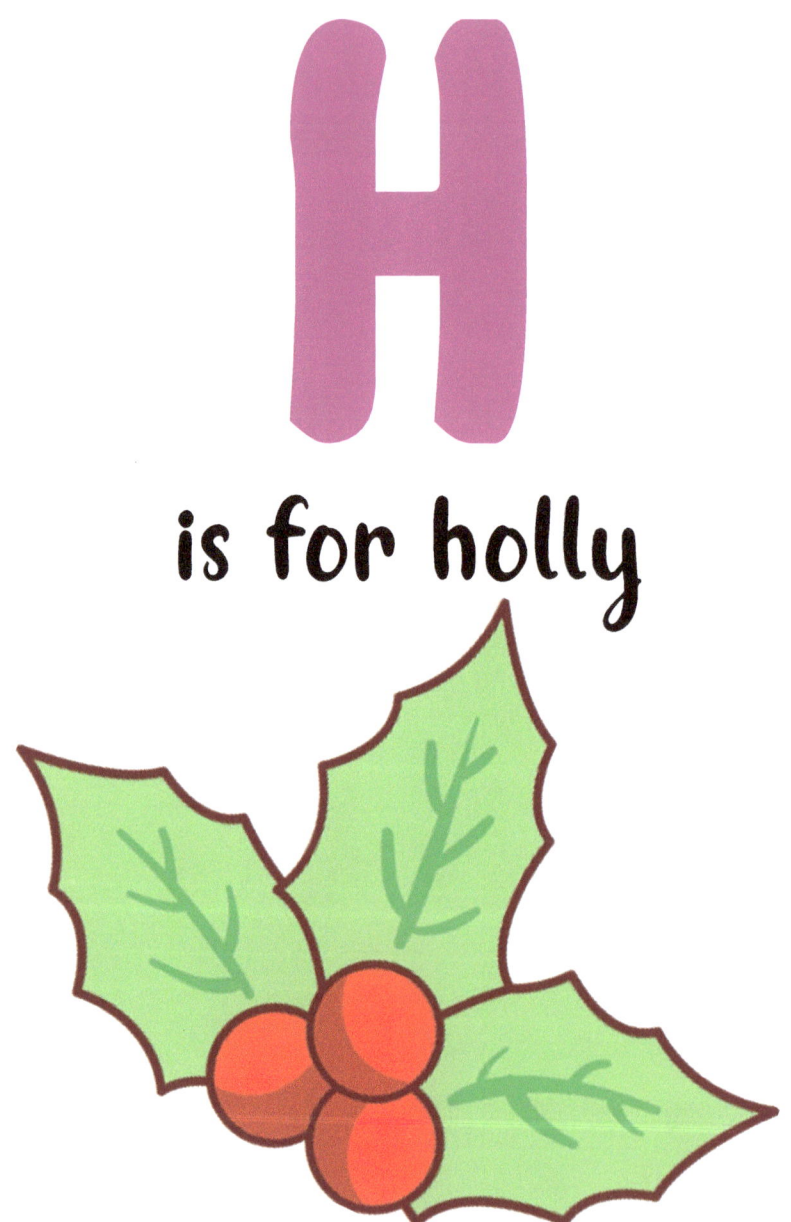

I SPY WITH MY LITTLE EYE ...
something beginning with ...

S

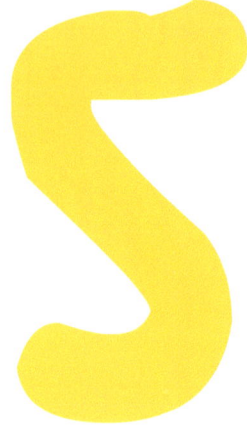

is for snowflake

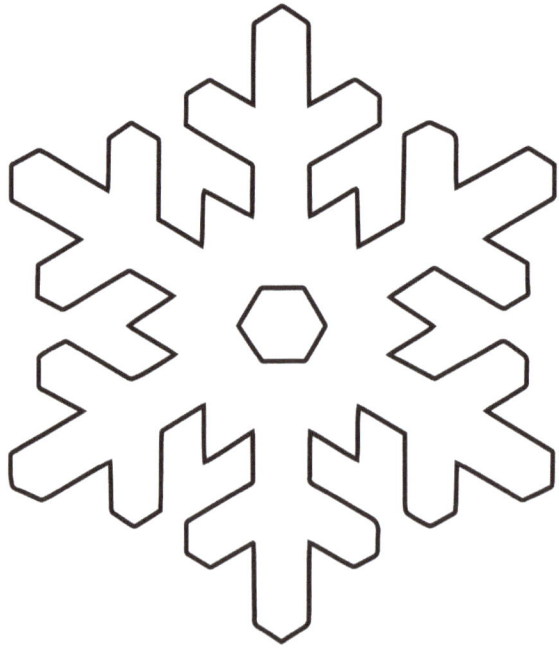

I SPY WITH MY LITTLE EYE ...
something beginning with ...

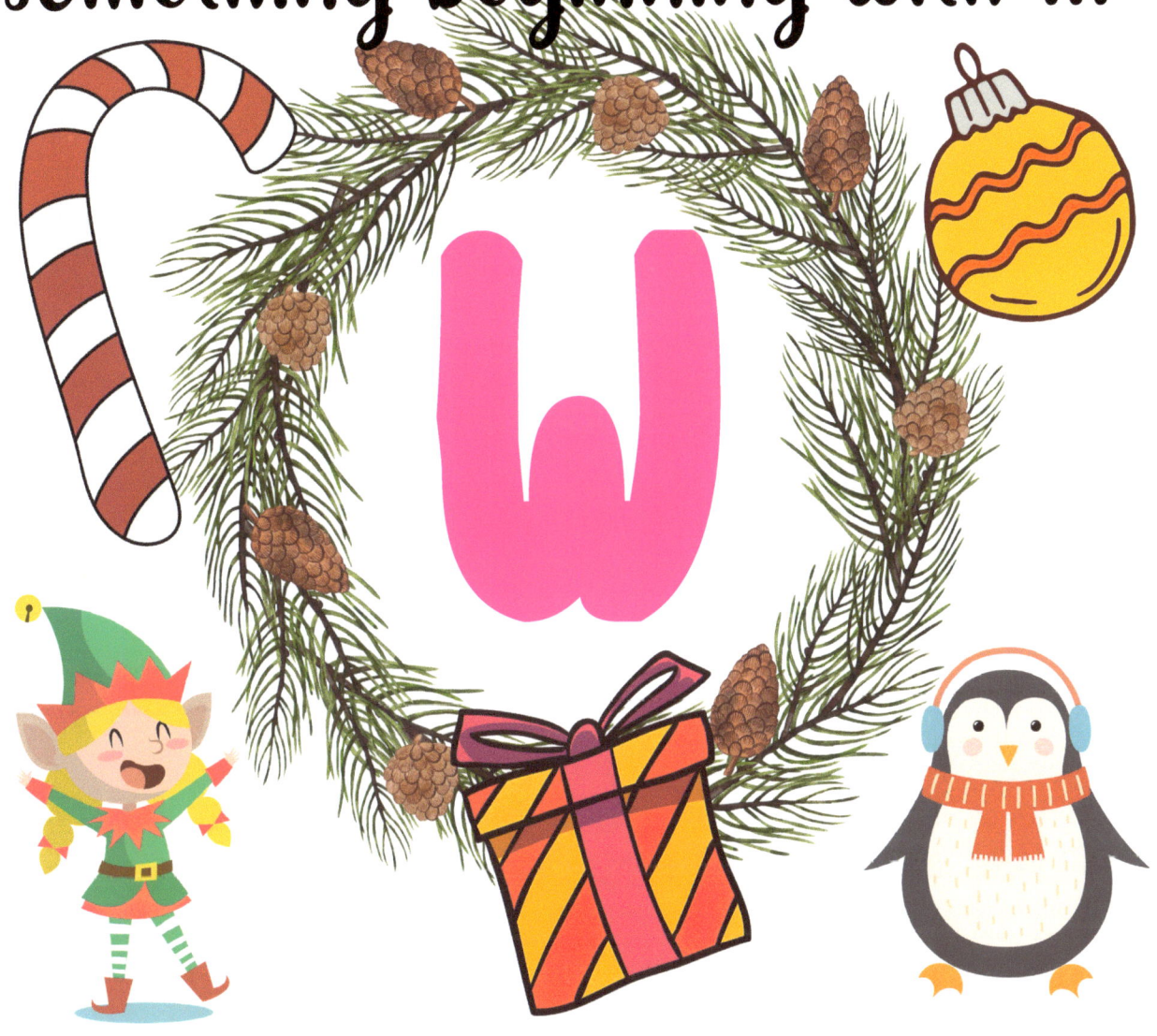

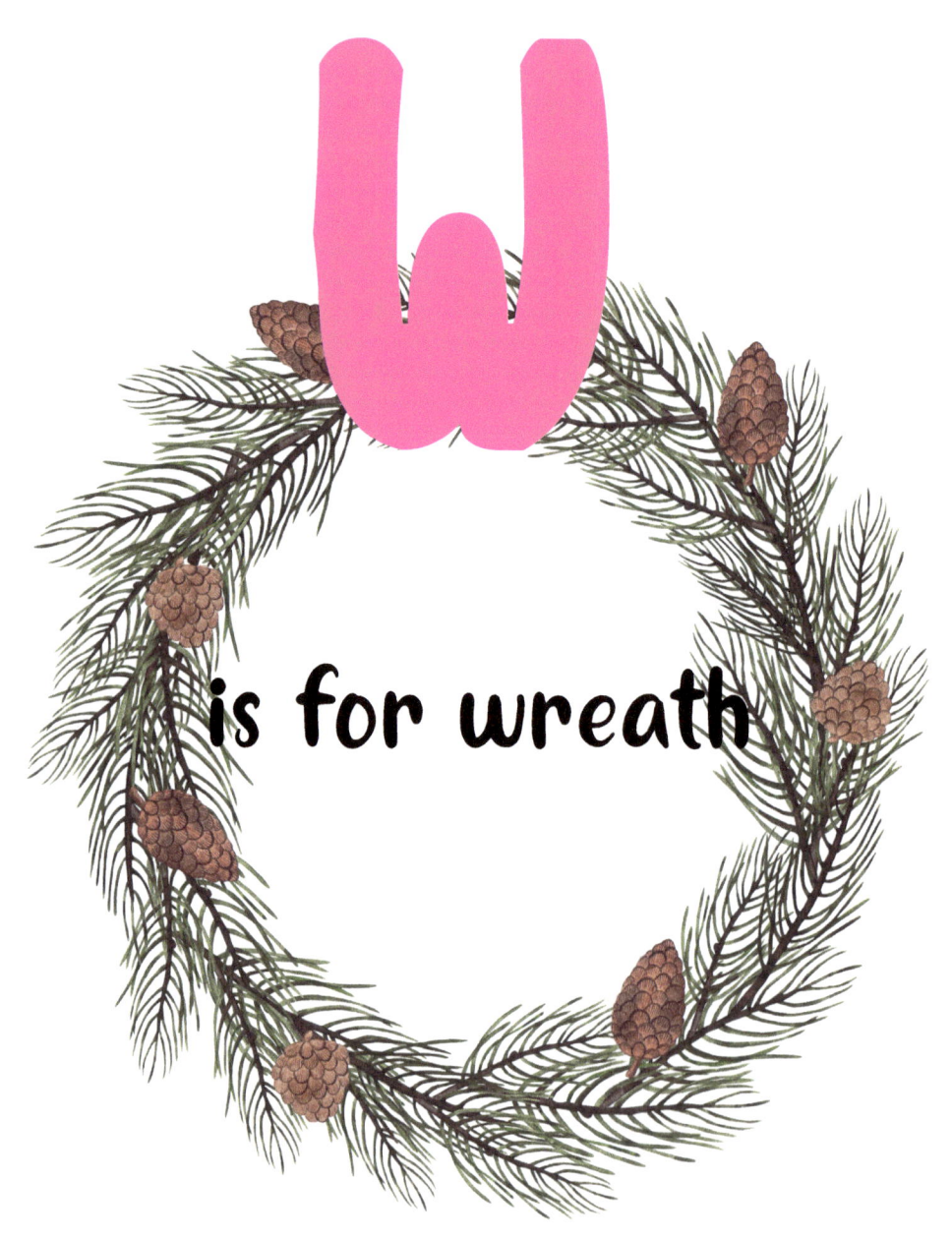
W is for wreath

I SPY WITH MY LITTLE EYE ... something beginning with ...

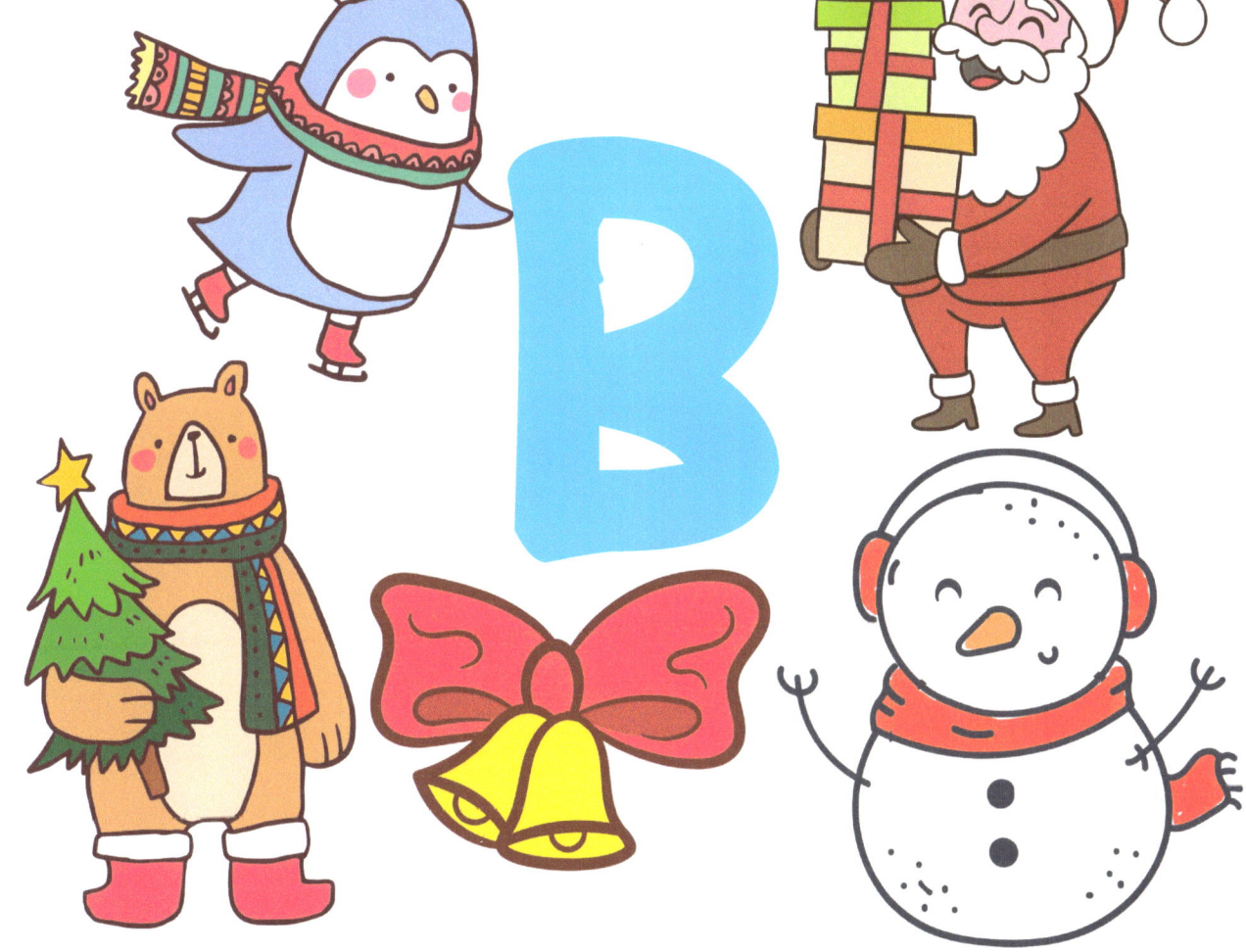

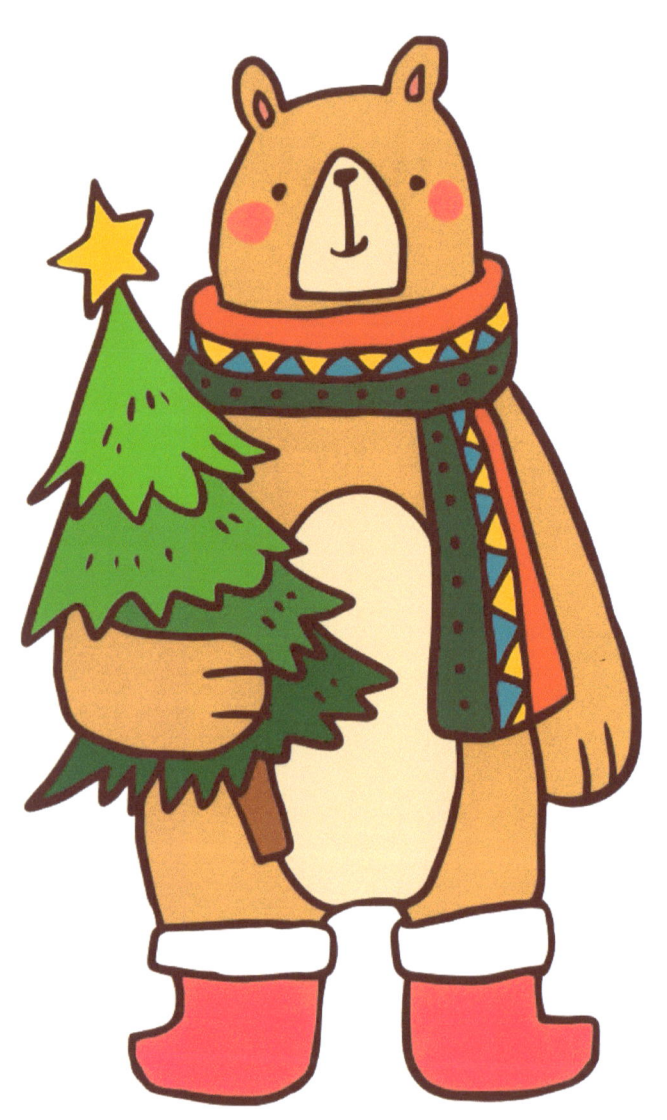 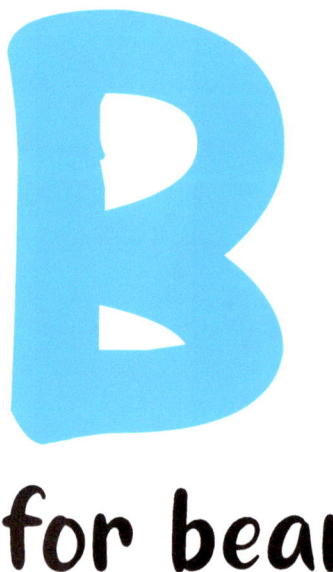

is for bear

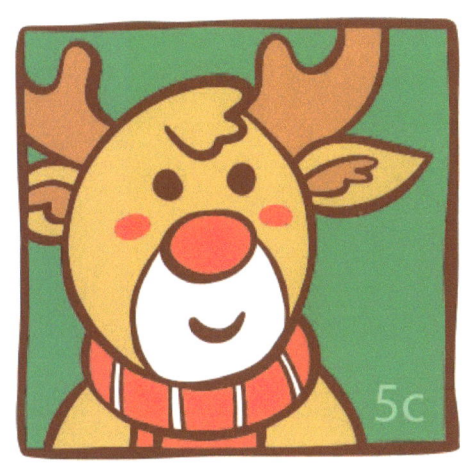
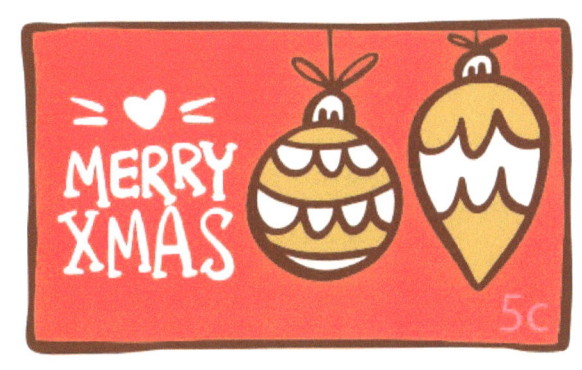

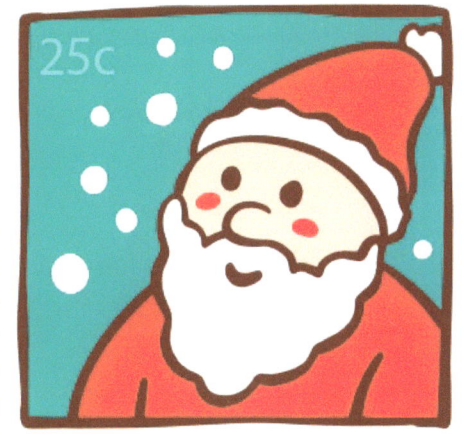
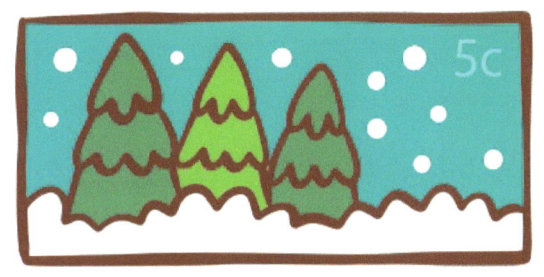

www.ingramcontent.com/pod-product-compliance
Lightning Source LLC
Chambersburg PA
CBHW040410220526
45473CB00004B/1192